Laurence Henry Schwab

The Kingdom of God

An Essay in Theology

Laurence Henry Schwab

The Kingdom of God

An Essay in Theology

ISBN/EAN: 9783337169060

Printed in Europe, USA, Canada, Australia, Japan

Cover: Foto ©Lupo / pixelio.de

More available books at **www.hansebooks.com**

THE KINGDOM OF GOD

AN ESSAY IN THEOLOGY

THE BOHLEN LECTURES, 1897

BY

LAURENCE HENRY SCHWAB

Rector of St. Mary's Church, New York

"In matters which concern the actions of God, the most dutiful way on our part is to search what God hath done, and with meekness to admire that, rather than to dispute what he in congruity of reason ought to do."—RICHARD HOOKER.

NEW YORK
E. P. DUTTON AND COMPANY
31 WEST TWENTY-THIRD STREET
1897

The Knickerbocker Press, New York

THE JOHN BOHLEN LECTURESHIP.

JOHN BOHLEN, who died in Philadelphia on the 26th day of April, 1874, bequeathed to trustees a fund of One Hundred Thousand Dollars, to be distributed to religious and charitable objects in accordance with the well-known wishes of the testator.

By a deed of trust, executed June 2, 1875, the trustees, under the will of MR. BOHLEN, transferred and paid over to " The Rector, Church Wardens, and Vestrymen of the Church of the Holy Trinity, Philadelphia," in trust, a sum of money for certain designated purposes, out of which fund the sum of Ten Thousand Dollars was set apart for the endowment of THE JOHN BOHLEN LECTURESHIP, upon the following terms and conditions:

"The money shall be invested in good, substantial, and safe securities, and held in trust for a fund to be called The John Bohlen Lectureship, and the income shall be applied annually to the payment of a qualified person, whether clergyman or layman, for the delivery and publication of at least one hundred copies of two or more lecture-sermons. These lectures shall be delivered at such time and place, in the city of Philadelphia, as the persons nominated to appoint the lecturer shall from time to time determine, giving at least six months' notice to the person appointed to deliver the same, when the same may conveniently be done, and in no case selecting the same person as lecturer a second time within a period of five years. The payment shall be made to said lecturer, after the lectures have been printed and received by the trustees, of all the income for the year derived from said fund, after defraying the expense of printing the lectures and the other incidental expenses attending the same.

"The subject of such lectures shall be such as is within the terms set forth in the will of the Rev. John Bampton, for the delivery of what are known as the 'Bampton Lectures,' at Oxford, or any other subject distinctively connected with or relating to the Christian Religion.

"The lecturer shall be appointed annually in the month of May, or as soon thereafter as can conveniently be done, by the persons who for the time being shall hold the offices of Bishop of the Protestant Episcopal Church of the Diocese in which is the Church of the Holy Trinity; the Rector of said Church; the Professor of Biblical Learning, the Professor of Systematic Divinity, and the Professor of Ecclesiastical History, in the Divinity School of the Protestant Episcopal Church in Philadelphia.

"In case either of said offices are vacant, the others may nominate the lecturer."

Under this trust, the Rev. L. H. Schwab was appointed to deliver the lectures for the year 1897.

TO MY WIFE

CONTENTS.

INTRODUCTION.

	PAGE
"The kingdom of God"	1
Christ's nature and his work distinguished	1
Theoretical and religious judgments	3–13
Theories of cognition and psychology	13–15
The question of a "proof" of Christianity	16–18

CHAPTER I.
THE RELIGIOUS DETERMINATION OF THE CHRISTIAN LIFE.

The eternal life	19–24
Man's relation to God	24–30
Sin	30–42
Forgiveness	42–49
Forgiveness not indifference	49–51

CHAPTER II.
THE ATONEMENT.

Forgiveness and justification	52–54
Forgiveness, a synthetic judgment	54
God forgives as Father	55
The Church as the object of forgiveness	57–60
Faith as the act of man	60–62
Forgiveness, the constitutive principle of Christianity	62–64
Forgiveness through Christ	65–85
Christ as a mere preacher of forgiveness	66–70
Theories of the atonement	70–85
The "imitation" of Christ	85–87

CHAPTER III.
THE ETERNAL LIFE.

Peculiarity of the Christian life—its scope	88–92
The "eternal life" in the New Testament	92–96
"Optimism"	96
Christian mastery	97–100
Mysticism	100–103
Natural and revealed religion	103
Christianity, the upholder of modern civilization	105–113
The Church's function—worship	113–119
The poets as Christian seers	119–122

CHAPTER IV.
THE IDEA OF GOD.

The value-tests and the metaphysical idea of God	123–129
The moral argument	129–136
Evil in its relation to the idea of God	136
Argument from beauty	137–140

	PAGE
Revelation. Dualism in the idea of God	140-143
Efforts to surmount the dualism	143-148
God as arbitrary will	148-150
Conditions for the solution of the problem of God	150-152

CHAPTER V.
THE IDEA OF GOD. *(Continued).*

Metaphysics and religion	153-161
God as love and the kingdom of God as the object of God's love	161-180
Freedom of the will	180-182
The necessity of the Christian idea of God	182-186
Theory and practice.	186-188

CHAPTER VI.
THE PERSON OF CHRIST.

The authenticity of the Gospels	189-194
The question of the supernatural	194-202
The divinity of Christ—conditions for the solution of the problem	202-210
The divinity of Christ: definition	211-219

CHAPTER VII.
THE ETHICAL DETERMINATION OF THE CHRISTIAN LIFE.

The dualism of the Christian life		220-228
The final authority		228-246
Biblical authority—		
I. Methods of study	231-236	
II. The results	236-239	
III. The bearings of these results	239-243	
The supreme authority of God	243-246	
The variableness of Christian ethics		246-249

CHAPTER VIII.
THE KINGDOM OF GOD AND THE STATE.

The Christian ethics distinguished by positiveness. The law of duty		250-256
The Church and the social question		256-258
The Church and the State		258-271
The State in its relation to the kingdom of God	258-262	
The Church in its relation to the State	262	
The Christian attitude	262-264	
The State and the principle of proportional responsibility	264	
Liberty and equality	264-267	
Where the responsibility lies	267-269	
The Church's opportunity	269-271	
The kingdom of God and the kingdom of the pope		271-276

PREFACE.

THIS book owes its being to two causes: to the invitation which I received to deliver the Bohlen Lectures in the winter of 1897 (they appear here somewhat amended and amplified); and to the inspiration I have derived from Albrecht Ritschl's great work on *Justification and Reconciliation*.

It would not be fair to make Ritschl responsible for all that I have written. Considerable portions are independent of Ritschl, in certain parts I have ventured to disagree with him, and in the last two chapters I have entered upon subjects which Ritschl hardly touches. Nevertheless, the main trend of thought and the method are Ritschlian.

I have not aimed at giving an exposition or a criticism of Ritschl. If these pages have any value, it comes from the mental appropriation of certain great truths in the exigencies of a profession which finds itself constantly confronted and challenged by the mystery of human life. These things are in the air, and I shall never forget my pleasure when, many years ago, I found Ritschl made those words of Christ the corner-stone of his system, which had long stood out in my mind as perhaps the most significant he uttered: " If any man will do his will, he shall know of the doctrine, whether it be of God, or whether I speak of myself."

Ritschl's critics have been right in distinguishing his attitude towards metaphysics as the crucial point of his system, but have generally, I think, done him something less than justice. I have become more and more assured in the conviction that his position is well taken. I have endeavoured to make that position clear, and I should like to hope that it might be my privilege to convince some, to whom the problems of theology are a matter of vital concern, that there is something in Ritschl's contention which is worth their thoughtful and sober consideration. The system of one, concerning whom it could be said " The joy of preaching the gospel entire and alone has been awakened by no theologian of the past decades to a greater degree than by Ritschl " (Nippold), cannot be overlooked by the intelligent and ought to be above the sarcasm with which its critics have sometimes thought to refute it.

A friend, whose opinion I highly value, when I undertook this work wrote to me about the subject: " I do not doubt you will treat it not as a finality." The words set me thinking. A claim to finality would indicate arrant conceit in whoever made it, and yet we should never lose sight of the fact that there is such a thing as finality in truth. All contemporary thought is under the influence of the historical spirit, which is dominant in the intellectual sphere; and it is one of the serious faults of Ritschl's writing that he fails clearly to distinguish between the historical and the philosophical, or religious, ideal.

The historical ideal is the complete and satisfactory exposition of the genetic development of beliefs, institutions, etc. It takes no account whatever of the inherent truth. The philosophical and religious ideal on the other hand is the pure fact, the absolute truth. The two are wide apart, and the theologian looks upon the historical as a means to the end; he will keep his eye fixed on the " finality," the absolute truth.

It is idle to suppose that we shall ever reach that finality. I do not share that confidence in our mental powers which anticipates any close approach to ultimate truth. Our best efforts are but a re-adjustment of the glasses. We see things in another light from those who went before; and those who come after us will again see differently, perhaps not more truly, but differently, because they will be under different influences. In one sphere only may we look for any marked approximation to an ultimate standard: the ethical.

But, whatever the prospect, there can be no doubt that a healthy spiritual life demands that we exert to the utmost such faculties as God has given us. The task is an unending one. Just now there seems to be a call for a forward movement in theology. Most of our mental energy has for the past fifty years or more been given to the correcting of mistakes and prejudices. The critical faculty has had its day. But now the problems of criticism are at least so far solved as to have brought out in clear relief certain principles, upon which it is possible to base a forward movement. The work of the coming years must be constructive. The task committed to us is to build up. Here Ritschl's work is undoubtedly epoch-making. To quote once more from the distinguished historian of the modern Church—himself not altogether a friendly critic: " For a vast number, who in the age of Darwin had lost courage for the task, he has once more confirmed their faith in the mission, which theology again claims as her own, to be a leader in the sphere of knowledge."

Theological science to-day calls for the best efforts of those who believe in the power of religion, and the call is not so much for brilliant intuitions, splendid guesses at the truth, as for patient, careful, painstaking, consecutive thought. There is no such thing as " finality " on this earth. But none the less is there imposed upon us the necessity of pressing toward the goal—

"Our hearts wide open on the Godward side."

INTRODUCTION.

CHRIST began his mission by preaching the advent of the Kingdom of God: "The time is fulfilled and the kingdom of God is at hand." In other versions it is "the kingdom of heaven." But this is probably a modification of the original expression, dating from a later time when the heavenly consummation of the kingdom became the uppermost thought.

"The Kingdom of Christ" stands historically for a different conception. This term dates from Puritan times, when it was used to designate that ecclesiastical organisation in which Puritanism found the outward expression of Christ's kingship.

Our interest is with the expression originally used by Christ: the kingdom of God. Christ did not create it, but found it as an essential element of the Jewish religion, and he began his mission with the full consciousness of being the Messiah appointed to bring in the fulfilment of that which had been foreshadowed by law and prophet in the Old Testament. Hence the kingdom of God is, as it were, the framework of Christ's mission. I shall endeavour to show how the several elements fit into this framework.

Our interest is in what Christ did rather than in what he was. It is worth while at the beginning of our enquiry to call attention to the difference. One view—it was especially the tendency of the early Greek theology—finds the significance of Christ in that which he was, in his nature. The Incarnation became the chief doctrine. Christ has sanctified human nature. He became man that man might become divine. It was a mystical-materialistic conception. God's nature joined itself to man's, took upon itself humanity: this miraculous process miraculously changed man's nature. The reconciliation between God and man meant a reconciliation of nature apart from will. Ethical considerations were left out. The consequences of this theory were equally materialistic. Religion came to mean an elaborate system of mysteries, charms, ceremonies, by which the fruition of heavenly things was attained. The Church degenerated into a mechanism for supplying these requisites of salvation. Christianity became paganised.

On the other hand, the interest in what Christ *did* for man opens the door for the ethical. His significance to the world lay in the quality of his actions. The reconciliation between God and man is the reconciliation of the will, and the great spiritual truths assume their place in the Christian system: righteousness, the love of God in Christ, justification, faith.) To the reaction from the Greek theology which St. Augustine inaugurated we owe it that these have been recognised as essential elements of Christian character. Our enquiry into the nature of the kingdom of God must follow these lines.

"So soon," says Lowell, "as an earnest conviction has cooled into a phrase, its work is over, and the best that can be done with it is to bury it." Religious truth was at first an earnest conviction. The history of theology proves that it has been apt to cool into a phrase. It then becomes a thing by itself, apart from experience, which may be dealt with according to its own laws. Theology degenerates into a mere fence of logic. This makes so many volumes of theological literature such dreary, profitless, and unconvincing reading. Mr. Gore, in the preface to his Bampton Lectures, states the principle which alone can guard us from the danger: "All right theory emerges out of experience and is the analysis of experience . . . the right method of philosophy is not *à priori*, abstract, or external, but is based in each department of enquiry upon a profound and sympathetic study of the facts." These words point in the direction of a truth which is of essential importance for our enquiry. Experience involves something more than intellect, and whoever takes experience for his guide cannot confine himself to mere logical process. The assumption made in behalf of an unprejudiced judgment, that the intellect is the only arbiter of truth, is false, and the pretended disinterestedness in matters of religion is an illusion.

The acquisition of knowledge is made by means of mental judgments. These judgments are formed by the mind working upon the sensations excited in the consciousness. In the act of judging, the mind appropriates or takes within itself its sensations.

This act of mental appropriation takes place in two ways. In one case, the feelings which are a part of the sensations are the determining factor; they indicate whether the particular sensations are helpful and therefore acceptable, or the reverse. I judge by the feelings. In the other case the feelings play no such part; the sensations serve to classify objects according to their origin, character, and connection with other objects—as is done in all scientific reasoning.

The judgments by the feelings are what Ritschl calls "value-judgments." Their operation will require some further explanation.

It may be laid down as a general truth that in no act of attentive reasoning is the intellect alone operative. An act of the pure intellect cannot be conceived except in dreams either waking or sleeping and possibly in the case of insane persons. The intellect used in reasoning is at all times subject to the will; the will is the determining, guiding factor in all mental operations. But the will never acts unless prompted by a motive, and this motive is in the shape of a feeling. Feeling is also present as an accompanying factor in every mental process. There is therefore no act of the mind without will and without feeling. For the proof of this state to yourself any proposition. Twice two is four: so far from the statement of this truth being a purely intellectual act, it is accompanied both by will and by feeling. For you would not say it, unless you were prompted to say it; therefore you will it. With the statement also goes a certain feeling, namely one of satisfaction, and this is the warrant that it is true. We may observe the absence of this feeling in the case of a false statement. Say to yourself: twice two is five—a distinct feeling of dissatisfaction accompanies that statement.

Feeling enters into every judgment which the mind makes. But there is a great difference in the various mental operations. In what we may call theoretical knowledge, in all scientific reasoning, the feelings are merely regulative: they fix the attention, they give their approbation or disapprobation of the result. They have no power in themselves to affect the judgment. But there is a large class of mental judgments in which the function of the feeling in the act of judging is far more important, in which the feeling has a great deal to do in determining the judgment. This may be readily illustrated by the moral judgments. It is wrong to kill. In so far as this judgment is addressed to the intellect, it is put in terms of the intellect. It is a proposition submitted to your mind like any other proposition. But in the act of mental appropriation by which that statement becomes a subjective judgment, what is the determining influence? It is not intellectual, it is moral. This is therefore a value-judgment proper, in which the value of the moral feelings which go with the mental process determine the acceptation of the statement as truth. You believe the statement because you believe your feelings.

It is because of this peculiarity in the quality of moral judgments that we differentiate moral truth from theoretical truth. It is by an analogous peculiarity of our religious judgments that we also differentiate religious truth. The value-judgments hold in religion as well as in morals. In religious judgments our feelings not only may, but must be given decisive weight. It is a fundamental mistake, an error which has caused the greatest confusion of thought, to set up the law of theoretical knowledge as the law of the human spirit in all its various functions. An unbiassed, unprejudiced, purely objective and intellectual proof of Christianity has been challenged by its enemies and eagerly sought by its champions, with equal disregard of the truth that the faith which prompts the one to defend religion and the disbelief which moves the other to attack it are not the result of logical methods of reasoning. Therefore the efforts of the one to uphold and of the other to destroy faith by such methods must prove alike disappointing.

The difference between the logical method of dealing with religious truth and the one which is here advocated can hardly be overestimated. I have endeavoured to show the nature of moral judgments. Religious judgments also are influenced by the moral feelings. But the value-judgments which especially belong to the religious sphere are different. Their exact nature will, I trust, be made clear in the course of this enquiry. At this point it will be proper merely to indicate the objects with which the religious judgments have to do and to point out the form of their operation.

The objects with which an enquirer into the nature of the Christian religion will concern himself are such as: God, Christ, the eternal life, heaven, salvation, justification, the kingdom of God. Theology defines them, seeks to determine the modes of their operation and to harmonise them. Theoretical enquiry pretends to have no personal interest in these things and undertakes to define and determine them according to their nature, independently of any value which they may have for man. The theological enquirer cannot set aside this value and his interest in it; to him this very interest is a factor in determining and defining the objects. He does not much care to know what God may be in himself, but he wants to know what God is *for him*. That which God is for man is the thing upon which he fixes his attention. If I believe in God, I believe in him, not because the metaphysician has proved to me the existence of God, but because I need God, because God means something for me. This *for me* represents the contents of the value-judgment which I form of God. The same is true of other objects of theological interest.

It must be borne in mind that we are rarely conscious of our mental operation in forming judgments, but theological differentiates itself from theoretical or metaphysical reasoning by being permeated by the sense of value inherent in the things about which it reasons. The difference goes to the foundation of our views of religion.

The method which is here advocated finds its confirmation in the words of Christ, St. John vii. 17: "If any man will do his will, he shall know of the doctrine, whether it be of God or whether I speak of myself." Christ here makes the exercise of the will a factor in probing the truth of his doctrine. It will be readily seen that the application of this principle is incompatible with the prosecution of mere logical or intellectual methods of enquiry into the nature of Christianity.[1]

It follows from this that no judgment can properly be pronounced upon Christianity from without. Whoever would have a clear perception of what Christianity is must have measured by his own experience its spiritual value. The experience of this value, the appreciation of what Christianity is for man, one gets only as a Christian, as a follower of Christ. To occupy any other position would be to yield to the fatal illusion which under the name of historical disinterestedness has distorted the religious judgment.

[1] "We see then as we feel—

. . . .

And in your judgment, Sir, the mind's repose
On evidence is not to be ensured
By act of naked reason. Moral truth
Is no mechanic structure, built by rule :
And which, once built, retains a steadfast shape
And undisturbed proportions ; but a thing
Subject, you deem, to vital accidents ;
And, like the water-lily, lives and thrives,
Whose root is fixed in stable earth, whose head
Floats on the tossing waves."
The Excursion, Book V.

There are objections to this method which we may briefly glance at. It will be said that it makes selfishness the criterion of truth. The lack of a proper discrimination in the use of this word has been the cause of much mischief. Without some sort of selfishness life would be absolutely impossible. If to exalt the value of my individual personal life is selfish, then Christianity is the most selfish religion; for Christ teaches the infinite worth of human life. Selfishness, in the bad sense, consists in the opposition of the individual to the common interests of humanity. What may be called Christian selfishness is self-respect and a high valuation of my own personality. So far from being opposed to the common interests, it is inconceivable apart from a due regard for the interests of others.

Some slight reflection will make clear the fruitlessness of the efforts which are made to reduce life to what is conceived as pure unselfishness. When one has divested himself of all "selfish" motives and has supplanted the interest in self by the engrossing interest in others' welfare, there remains as an ineradicable element of the process the inner satisfaction with one's actions. This is the only conceivable motive of the most unselfish conduct. So it is selfish after all. Only the person tries to deceive himself into believing that he has cast self aside. No wonder that the result is commonly the most offensive form of selfishness: spiritual self-righteousness.

Again, it will be objected that this method makes religious judgment a mere subjective matter, subject to the caprice and the whims of the individual. There is here some confusion of thought. What mental process is there which is not " subjective " ? How is any judgment of the individual conceivable except as subjective, that is, as formed through the processes of his own, not other's mind ? It may be urged that the feelings and the will, upon which this theory lays the emphasis, are more subject to vagaries and aberrations than the intellect. But in view of the existing diversities in matters of religion which are mere differences of opinion, this can hardly be maintained.

The true bearing of this objection on the ground of subjectivity lies in another direction. The conception of belief has undergone a considerable change in the Christian Church. In the early ages it was the belief in certain life-saving truths. The faith in the second coming of Christ, the trust in a God of love, the father of our Lord Jesus Christ; such were the beliefs that sustained the early Christians in the battle with the world. But the πίστις slowly gave way to the γνῶσις. The conclusions drawn from the first articles of faith became more and more elaborated, and a belief in these theological elaborations became a condition of membership in the Christian Church. Ordinary minds were incapable of independent judgment. Nevertheless they gave their assent, and this they did by expressing their belief in a creed. This meant for the vast majority of people the substitution for the belief in truth of a belief in a belief. The belief itself became the object of credence; and faith has ever since been commonly judged as the act of assent to a creed, the belief in a belief. Contrasted with this, it is acknowledged that the theory here advocated has a tendency to make religion "subjective," in the sense of bringing the great Christian truths directly home to the mind.[1]

Christianity cannot be appreciated in its true nature, unless it is understood that the sphere of the spiritual lies above and beyond the natural, and that it has its own laws which are different from the laws of nature. The conflicts between science and religion have been caused by the false assumption that the laws which govern in that limited portion of the universe, which we call the natural world, are valid for the entire universe. Upon this assumption science has demanded of religion proofs for the validity of its claims. Such proofs, let it be understood, religion is unable to give and should not attempt to give. For what would the attempt mean? It would imply the possibility of measuring Christianity by a standard belonging to another sphere whose

[1] Ernest Renan had a certain realisation of the truth of the position here taken. No person, he claims, can be a judge of Christianity who has not himself been a Christian. But, he adds, he must have ceased to be a Christian to be an impartial judge. On the score of disinterestedness such a position has no claim superior to the one here taken. The person who has made up his mind that Christianity is untrue is not more impartial than the believer. It is an interesting study to discover the prejudice which clouded the vision of so eminent a critic of Christianity as Renan. A glance at his picture does it in his case. It explains the psychological puzzle of the author of the *Vie de Jesus* and *L'Abbesse de Jouarre*.

laws are different from those of its own. As well might the musician measure the value of musical compositions with the yard-stick. Philosophy has its proper sphere and the laws belonging to it. Science has its sphere, and the laws of that sphere are absolutely binding to the scientific enquirer. But the sphere and the laws of philosophy are not those of religion, and the sphere and the laws of science are not those of religion.

It is a common fault of theological reasoning that it fails to grasp this distinction. When Christ taught the transcendent value of the soul, the essential difference between man and the world, he set before man a new truth of the most far-reaching character. Of that truth pagan philosophy had no conception. But Christian theology would seem to have been influenced more by Greek philosophy in its attempt to explain the Cosmos than by the new truth of Christ. It gave to pagan philosophy a home in the Christian system and strove for the knowledge of the conditions of all being after the methods of the ancient wisdom. At the top of the system thus constructed it added the truths of Redemption. This incongruous mixture of pagan cosmology and Christian soteriology was accepted as Christian philosophy. But it was Christian only in the sense of being dressed with a few Christian truths; it was not Christian in that it neglected the fundamental distinction which Christianity made between man and nature, between the Ethos and the Cosmos, and the inevitable consequences which this distinction entails upon our views of the world.

These conditions of theological investigation are fundamental and affect the whole conception of Christian truth. Just as with natural objects the truth of our perceptions often depends upon the light in which we see them, so in theology. It is of the first importance that at the opening of a theological enquiry one get into the proper light. If you have succeeded in doing that, half the battle is won, the rest will follow naturally. And this first condition is satisfied by learning to appreciate the essential difference between theoretical and religious knowledge.

There remains one more subject which I must here treat of, which is also fundamental to our investigation: the proper theory of cognition and of psychology. When we say we know a thing, what do we mean? Plato taught that a thing is composed of a "substance" and the "accidents." This Platonic "substance" was a delusion of the intellect. It had its origin in that process of unification, by which the mind combines the effects upon the various sense organs produced by contact with an object.

Kant showed that the thing in itself is, in its nature, unknowable; all that we can know is phenomena. We know the thing itself only as the cause of the phenomena by which it comes into contact with our faculties. This theory of cognition forbids any further enquiry into the nature of the thing itself. The application of this metaphysical doctrine to theology is of the first importance. Scarcely anything has been so productive of evil in theological speculation as the Platonic doctrine of universals. These universals were removed from human observation, but not from human speculation. Accordingly fancy was free to play with them at will. Any absurdity might be predicated of the "substance," however contradictory to the known laws of the accidents. The baneful influence of this theory is manifest in its application to the doctrine of God. Men were not satisfied to know God as Christ revealed him. They sought to fathom the reality underneath the divine manifestations, and lost themselves in fruitless speculations.[1]

With the acceptance of the Kantian theory of cognition we impose upon ourselves certain limitations of knowledge which it is highly necessary in a theological investigation to bear in mind.

Theology demands not only a correct epistemology, but also a correct psychology. Analogous to the distinction between substance and accident is the theory which ascribes to the soul a life behind its activities. Back of the feeling, the will and the knowing, is the soul itself. Not only is the will of man sanctified and his mind inspired and his feelings transmuted

---

[1] The application of the Platonic theory to the doctrine of the Holy Communion is the most striking instance of its abuse. Theological caprice has fairly run riot in dealing with the "substance" and the "attributes" of Christ's body. Self-contradictory miracles, which no sane mind could assert of anything real that had ever been seen in the world, were accepted with perfect equanimity when applied to that mysterious entity, a "substance."

by the influence of God, but behind these is the union of the soul itself with the divine, and manifestations of this union are sought outside of the soul's ordinary activities.

But we cannot get to the soul behind its activities. As soon as we know anything of the soul, it is the soul as feeling, willing, or knowing. If God is united to the soul, the only intelligible meaning that can be attached to such a statement is that God has sanctified the faculties of the soul, producing harmony and peace where before was discord and unrest. The soul receives no impression as passive. Every impression received is met by a counter-activity of the soul itself. The only way the soul appropriates impressions is by having its own faculties stirred to activity. The pain which the soul feels is conceived only as its own activity; so with all other sensations. Therefore the attitude of the soul towards the grace of God is not simply receptive; grace is not poured into the soul as water into a vessel. Such a process is inconceivable. The grace of God in the human soul becomes the activity of the soul itself. Theology therefore has imposed upon it the task of tracing the dealings of God with man in the religious and ethical activities of the soul. We know the soul only in one of its functions, as feeling, willing, or knowing.[1]

[1] Some psychologists, I believe, reduce the soul to a series of "psychic processes." But they are not agreed. Until the matter is settled, we will retain the old phraseology. If necessary, we shall learn without much difficulty to say: "My psychic processes are athirst for God, yea even for the living God."

I have said that to attempt to prove Christianity, in the ordinary meaning of that word, is to attempt the impossible. It is a Sisyphus labour upon which the Christian mind has spent untold effort. The facts of the Christian revelation may be fortified by evidence; certain considerations may be adduced, as Bishop Butler has done, to make the Christian truth appear in accord with the system of the universe as it is known to us. All this does not lift Christian truth beyond the sphere of the probable. But the faith which is not raised above the balancing of probabilities is not a Christian faith. Hence this sort of effort has always been dissatisfying and discouraging to earnest enquiring minds.[1] To gain the strong conviction which reaches the level of true Christian faith another way must be taken. It must be by a spiritual appropriation of Christianity, as Christ

[1] That view of religion, which does not get beyond the "probability" stage, where the great object is to make yourself "safe" with God, rests upon a fundamental misconception. There is nothing more dreary than the picture of religion drawn by Arthur Hugh Clough. That which should be a support becomes a burden:

> " To spend uncounted years of pain,
>   Again, again and yet again,
>   In working out in heart and brain
>   The problem of our being here ;
>   To gather facts from far and near,
>   Upon the mind to hold them clear,
>   And, knowing more may yet appear,
>   Unto one's latest breath to fear
>   The premature result to draw—
>   Is this the object, end and law,
>   And purpose of our being here?"

pointed out: "If any man will do his will, he shall know of the doctrine whether it be of God or whether I speak of myself." If any proof of Christianity is possible, it can be only by showing that the highest aspirations of man are satisfied by Christianity and by that alone.

We are on one side of our nature bound to the lower creation. The same biological laws hold sway over us as over the brute, the same laws of growth and of death, the same struggle for existence and the same survival of the fittest. Turn your face in that direction, study man in his lower nature, and you recoil with horror as the picture reveals itself to you of man's life on earth. Looked at from this point of view, his history is little different from that of the other animals: universal selfishness, universal struggle. No wonder that men who have looked only on that side of the picture have said in despair, that as man shares his life with the brute, so he will share the brute's fate. But that is not all, there is another side. Whatever the ties are which bind man to the earth, there is also an affinity with heaven. If man is subject to the physical and chemical and biological laws which govern the universe, there are also other laws which reach down into his life from a higher sphere. You must take the whole of man, not one part of him. If you tell me that the laws of biology interpret his physical life, you must also find the laws which will interpret to me his higher life. Tell me whence his aspirations. Tell me the meaning of that

> ". . . Vexing, forward reaching sense,
> Of some more noble permanence."

Explain to me the spiritual life of man. That view of man which looks only to one side of his nature is miserably one-sided. The whole of man's life is greater than the laws of his physical being. There is in us an ineradicable sense that God could never have made man with these aspirations for something higher than this life affords, only in the end to bring him to utter confusion. Christianity is to us the warrant that these feelings are true; and if there is any proof which one can give to another of the Christian religion, it can only be the bringing up of man to the meeting point of man with God in Christ, the setting forth of Christianity as the one and only satisfaction for the soul's truest, deepest needs.

It follows from this that theology has its task distinctly defined. It is simply the analysis of the common Christian faith. Guided by this principle, I shall try to discover the outlines of that kingdom of God which Christ founded.

CHAPTER I.

THE RELIGIOUS DETERMINATION OF THE CHRISTIAN LIFE.

THE most cursory examination of the New Testament will make it evident that the revelation of truth contained in it is not homogeneous. There are elements in the teaching, both of Christ and of the apostles, which are not reduced to unity. The ethical teaching of Christ is patent on every page of the gospels. But this ethical element does not exhaust the significance of Christianity. Immediately following the Sermon on the Mount with its clear moral teaching, we find the story of the paralytic. It contains no ethical element, but something which has an entirely different bearing: the forgiveness of sins. A little farther on Jesus teaches his disciples to pray: " forgive us our trespasses."

Forgiveness is an element in the revelation of Jesus clearly distinct from the ethical. It has reference not so much to doing as to being; it has no direct application to conduct, but to a state. Many other words of Jesus have reference to a state in man. When we hear him calling to men, " Come unto me all ye who are weary and heavy laden," there is no question of right doing but of right being. So, too, with the numerous references in the Gospel of St. John to the " eternal life ": " This is eternal life—says Jesus—that they might know thee the only true God and Jesus Christ whom thou hast sent "; " I am come that they might have life." And again, when he prayed: " That they all may be one; as thou, Father, art in me, and I in thee, that they may be one in us." Or when in the last discourse he promises peace and joy: " Peace I leave with you, my peace I give unto you," " These things have I spoken unto you that my joy might remain in you, and that your joy might be full." Finally we have those expressions of our Lord asserting a purpose to his life and death, whose meaning a mere ethical explanation is wholly inadequate to exhaust: " The Son of man came to give his life a ransom for many," " This is my body which is given for you."

When we turn from the gospels to the epistles, we find this side of Christ's teaching fully represented. With St. Paul it is the main interest of Christianity. Something had freed him from the bondage of his former life; this something was not a code of morals; he felt himself redeemed from a slavish obedience to a law into a state of liberty in which he now glories. Christ now lives in him, he is justified, he is reconciled: such expressions find no explanation from mere ethical premises. Read the end of the eighth chapter of the Epistle to the Romans: " In all these things we are more than conquerors through him that loved us. For I am persuaded that neither death, nor life, nor angels, nor principalities, nor powers, nor things present, nor things to come, nor height, nor depth, nor any other creature, shall be able to separate us from the love of God, which is in Christ Jesus our Lord," or the closing words of the third chapter of First Corinthians: " All things are yours; whether Paul, or Apollos, or Cephas, or the world, or life, or death, or things present, or things to come; all are yours; and ye are Christ's, and Christ is God's ": no one can read such language and doubt that there entered into the life of the great apostle as chief determining factor something which cannot be summed up in a moral code.

Turning to other writers of the New Testament we find that St. Paul is by no means isolated in his conception of the nature of Christianity. We meet with such terms as " salvation " in the Epistle to the Hebrews, " propitiation " in those of St. John, and the frequent references to " overcoming " in the Revelation—all of them pointing to an element in the religion of Jesus which is something more than ethical.

It is not necessary to present an exhaustive summary of this factor in the New Testament teaching. It is too evident to need this. Or it ought to be too evident — too evident for the neglect with which it is not infrequently passed over. When Matthew Arnold tells us that " the object of religion is conduct," that religion is " morality touched by emotion,"[1] one is at a loss to understand how he, Bible-critic as he was, could have ignored all the religious element as distinct from the ethical in the Old and in the New Testament. To pretend to explain Christianity, while neglecting and setting aside that religious factor which was the strongest motive power in those who have left the most lasting impress upon the spiritual life of mankind, a St. Paul, a St. Augustine, a Luther; not even to attempt to account for the influences which most powerfully swayed these men: surely this is a strange historical criticism.[2]

How perfectly shallow a merely ethical conception of religion is will become still more evident by another consideration. We have a word in modern language for which there is no equivalent in the ancient tongues: that word is character. Character is distinctly a Christian conception; because Christianity alone furnishes the elements for its formation. The ancient world had very pronounced ethical ideas, but no combination of ethical qualities makes up character. You may conceive of a man as being just, kind, liberal, upright, and add all the virtues to the catalogue, and yet the sum of them all will fail to reach the fulness of what is meant when you speak of a man of character. The word is unex-

[1] *Literature and Dogma*, chap. i.
[2] Compare for a piece of historical criticism the following from *Literature and Dogma* (p. 78, Macmillan's edition): "Jesus Christ's new and different way of putting things was the secret of his succeeding where the prophets failed." One rubs his eyes and reads again. But there it stands.

plained upon the atomistic theory; it implies unity, an unfolding of life from within; it points to a centre of the spiritual nature. The use of the word character in popular language is a striking evidence of the moulding of our forms of thought through the influence of Christianity. The conception of a state of being antecedent to conduct, of a something in man from which conduct springs, a conception which owes its origin entirely to Christianity, has become so at home in popular thought as to be incorporated in every day language.

We observe furthermore about this word character, that there is a tendency to narrow its meaning, so that it is often used as implying that which is praiseworthy. We speak of a man " of character," meaning thereby strong or good character; or we say of another, " he is a man of no character." In this use of the word it comes very near in meaning to the expression used by Christ, already referred to: " the eternal life." We have been largely accustomed to think of the eternal life as something of the future, something different from this life, and yet Christ's assertions are most pronounced to the effect that it is of the present, a life for us to enter now: " This *is* eternal life, that they might know thee, the only true God "—" He that heareth my word, and believeth on him that sent me, *hath* everlasting life—*is passed* from death unto life " (St. John xvii. 3, v. 24). The difference between the earthly life and the eternal life is not one of quantity or duration, but of quality.

The word life in its meaning ranges over a most extensive scale. We apply to the worm crawling on the ground and to the highest perfection of Christian manhood equally the term life; but how different is life from life; how many the gradations from the lowest form, the simplest structure, through the life of instinct, of intelligence, of dawning conscience, of the perfected moral faculty, to that life which has attained to the highest nobility of character, to the full strength of independent fearless manhood, such as we see it only in a few illustrious examples. These gradations of life make us understand something of the truth underlying the expression "eternal life." In comparison with all other life, it is the highest, most perfect conceivable.

Only when we have grasped the conception which Christ embodied in the term "eternal life," are we in a position to understand something of human life on its God-ward side. The conception of religion as a set of rules for conduct seems beautifully simple. But is human life simple? The more we know of human nature, the more we stand in awe of its mystery. The deeper the insight into that strangest of earthly phenomena, the human heart, the more do we learn to appreciate the fact that there is a simplicity of shallowness.

There are two radically divergent views of life.[1] The one looks upon the surface, the other penetrates into the underlying realities. One man is

[1] It is a pity we have no word for the German "Weltvorstellung."

fascinated by the mechanism of the world; to understand its working is his absorbing object. To another the things of sense lack abiding reality; he feels for the eternal underneath. The one man is satisfied with secondary causes; to him, what he sees, the manifest connection between cause and effect, is sufficient. The other is always straining for the first cause; he feels himself in the presence of a great mystery; he cannot rest till he has found a clue to the problem. Fundamentally, the distinction between these two divergent views of life is this: God and no God. Not that the man who is a secularist in his interpretation of the world necessarily disbelieves in God; but if he does not bring his God to the explanation of the world, if he does not see the world around him in God's light, then he is practically without God. The theoretical acknowledgment of an absolute being, or by whatever other name you may choose to call it, is of no value. Either explain life through God, or put God aside where Jupiter and Osiris and the other deities of antiquity are.

Between the man to whom God is a practical necessity, to whom the world without God is a phantom, and another to whom this world is a godless world, although he may cap his materialistic philosophy with a conventional theoretical acknowledgment of a supreme being: between these two there can be no greater difference. The God-view and the godless view of life are diametrically opposed; there can be no harmony between them. The lines of this issue cannot be obliterated. It is God or no God.

It is not my purpose to prove the religious view of the world. I merely wish to point out the vast difference between the two views. The religious view of life assumes God as the necessary correlate of human life. The secular view of life is the self-centred, the Christian view, the God-centred life.

This will help to explain what Christ meant by the "eternal life." In his conception of that life God is the determining factor. He proves it in himself. What is more noticeable about the life of Jesus than his closeness to God: " No man knoweth the Son but the Father; neither knoweth any man the Father, save the Son, and he to whomsoever the Son will reveal him " (St. Matt. xi. 27)—" My meat is to do the will of him that sent me " (St. John iv. 34). It is unnecessary to quote any more. No fact is more patent. From childhood, when the consciousness of a higher relationship first dawned upon his mind and he felt the impulse to " be about his Father's business," to the cross, when the sense of being forsaken by God marked the deepest suffering, it is the same principle that shines through the years of Christ's earthly life, that of the closest dependence upon and union with God. Here perhaps more than anywhere else is seen the wretched inadequacy of all mere secular criteria of life. It is simply impossible to construe the life of Jesus without recognising the religious factor. You may say that his sense of oneness with God was a delusion; then this delusion was the mainstay, the fundamental principle of his life.

It will be furthermore evident that the object of Jesus was to extend that same life to his disciples. Thus he declares: " I am come that they might have life and that they might have it more abundantly " (St. John x. 10). And that this life is the same as his own, a life in God, he explains in his prayer: " That they all may be one; as thou, Father, art in me, and I in thee, that they also may be one in us." Hence the importance which he attaches to his own person, the invitations to come to him, to learn of him, to believe in him, his setting forth of himself as the way, the truth, and the life, the resurrection, the bread of life.

Now we are in a position more clearly to define that element in the New Testament which is distinct from the ethical. It is the religious determination of the Christian life. We use here the term religious in the stricter sense as denoting a relationship to God. The distinctively religious is what concerns man's relation to God, the ethical has not the same direct relationship to God. The ethical in man is his self-determination. The gospels contain no accurate definitions. But there is enough in the words of Christ and of the writers of the New Testament epistles to differentiate the religious from the ethical determination of the Christian life. We understand from the words of Christ that in his own case it consisted in the completest union between himself and God. For his followers we can conceive of this life only as an approach to that perfect union. The religious determination of the Christian life is nearness to God. This is figurative speech, and the analogy is taken from relations of space; but perhaps we can in no better way give expression in human imperfect language to the spiritual truth. We may also conceive that relationship as one of agreement of the will with God. The more we approach to the realisation of the eternal life, by so much we come nearer to God, or so much more does our will agree with that of God.

We have now found solid ground upon which to base our argument in the consideration of the kingdom of God. We have differentiated the religious from the ethical determination of the Christian life. The understanding of what follows will depend upon the clear appreciation of the distinction. In the kingdom of God which Christ established we find these two factors, the religious and the ethical. The consideration of the relationship between the two is reserved for a subsequent chapter. Here the distinction between them is the essential point. We insist upon this: antecedent to the ethical self-determination of man is the determination of his relationship to God. Before the doing there is a being, and that being consists in the union with God, or in the nearness to God. This is character as we use the word in our modern language. This is the eternal life as Christ used the expression. So he himself says: " This is eternal life that they might know thee the only true God and Jesus Christ whom thou hast sent " (St. John xvii. 3).

In one form or another the truth which is here

contended for has been the subject of ever-recurring disagreement among Christians. But here and there have risen men who have felt deeply that truth, whose souls have been a-fire with the sense of man's spiritual relationship to God, and wherever they have appeared they have profoundly stirred the hearts of their fellowmen. Such was St. Paul and such was St. Augustine. " If God be for us, who can be against us ? " said St. Paul. " Mihi adhærere deo bonum est " said St. Augustine. It was because of the grasp which these men had upon the religious determination of the Christian life that the motive power of every subsequent movement for the reformation of the Church is traced back to St. Augustine and through him to St. Paul.

It is therefore essential that we hold strongly to the determination of man's relationship to God before his ethical conduct. That view of religion which blurs the distinction between the ethical and the religious, which approaches more or less to the proposition I have cited, that " the object of religion is conduct," has always had a strong fascination, partly because of its supposed simplicity, largely because of the desire for unification of the two elements. It is instructive to notice the dogmatic decisions of the Council of Trent upon this subject. The fathers of the Council were not so blind to the distinctively religious factor as Mr. Matthew Arnold was, but their perplexity and consequent vacillation in bringing the ethical and the religious into proper relationship is very evident. This is seen in the decree on Justification.¹ The result is that in the Roman Catholic doctrine there is a recognition of God's relation to man in so far only as God's grace brings forth good works. The object is simply good works or conduct; there is no distinct recognition of a state of man in relation to God, which we call character, antecedent to conduct. The Christian life consists in good works. With us the Christian life consists primarily in our relation to God. By the neglect of this element there has been lost out of sight one of the essential aspects of Christian truth. The result may be read in the history of civilisation since the Council of Trent.²

Christ came to bring eternal life. Not conduct is the first object of Christianity, but life, that life which consists in the communion with God.

We, in the nineteenth century, are apt to think

[1] See Schaff's *Creeds of Christendom*.

[2] The decadence of Roman Catholic nations is doubtless due to the loss of virility and independence of character; and this again is due to the peculiar view of life favoured by the Church of Rome, which is theoretically expressed in its dogmas. In this age of depreciation of doctrine, it is essential to bear this fact in mind. A recent writer says: "And after all it has been justly said that the difference between the Roman doctrine and the Lutheran doctrine of justification is only the difference between a quæ and a qua. For my part I care as little for the quæ as for the qua" (Fulton, *The Calcedonian Decree*). There are two conceptions of theology. One is that of a science of accommodation to a burdensome yoke of dogma. The truer conception is that of the science of those spiritual forces which have operated upon Christian people and nations. It is this which gives importance to Christian doctrine and which makes the study of theology fascinating.

that we have discovered a universal solvent for all historical problems. The master-key which seems to unlock all mysteries is Evolution. It is not to be denied that we have received from such men as Darwin and Spencer a wonderful enlargement of the meaning of that term, which has brought new light into our conception of the world. But there is one stubborn fact connected with man which will not submit itself to the theory of evolution. Call that fact by whatever name you will, you will never get rid of the peculiar character attached to it by the old-fashioned name of Sin. From the elementary star-dust, through the lower up to the higher animal organisms, everything proceeds with the utmost regularity under the law of development, until you come to the creature man, who is endowed with the mysterious power of free-will, and with that faculty there comes sin. Sin enters into our subject because it is a bar to the realisation of that state which Christ described as man's destination, the eternal life. It must be very clear to the most ordinary observation, that man very generally fails of the realisation of even an approach to the life which we conceive as the ideal. The failure is too evident in the unhappiness, in the lack of purpose, in the restlessness, in the discontent, not to speak of the more obvious failures in pronounced selfishness and viciousness of life. We can all see that there is a disturbing element in life; life has missed its purpose, with many lamentably, with all to some degree. The disturbing element is sin. It is therefore essential at this point that we examine the Christian doctrine of sin.

The origin of sin is unessential to the Christian faith. Of that we have no knowledge. Whatever we may think of the story of the fall, it leaves the great mystery untouched. Why did God permit sin? The mind strives in vain and to no purpose to read this dark enigma. None who has a heart to feel the wickedness and the suffering in the world but will at times be oppressed with the weight of the mystery. But there are certain questions which we so plainly see to be beyond the grasp of human intelligence, that the wisest course for us is to set our faces resolutely away from them. We accept what we see, the fact that man has the power to make choice against his highest interests and that he is apparently governed by an inveterate propensity to make that evil choice. This power of choice seems to be a necessary condition of man's education. We must, however, beware of admitting any Manichæan dualistic theory. We cannot allow the possibility of an evil power outside of God, commensurate with his power. There is but one God.

The doctrine of sin has suffered from the metaphysical bias which has done so much harm in vitiating theological thought. It has been treated according to the realistic philosophy. St. Augustine stands as the exponent of an elaborate doctrine of sin, in which he gathered up the elements which seemed to him prerequisite to the Christian belief in redemption. We cannot here enter into a particular consideration of this theory or of the various modifications of it which have been proposed since the time of Augustine. It is sufficient if we recognise their common object and the fatal defects which characterise them alike. The object was to make all men partakers of sin and of its consequent amenability to punishment, by which the doom of death came upon the human race, and thereby to make redemption through Christ appear as necessary and rational. It was an attempt to justify God by means of a theory which in its nature was rationalistic. Men were not satisfied to take human nature where Christ took it, with its sinfulness and its need of a Redeemer. To establish a theory, St. Augustine forsook the Christian ground, repudiated the only criterion which Christians can acknowledge in religious things, and lost himself in a series of speculations whose forms were borrowed from an alien philosophy. The result of these speculations was then brought back into the sphere of religion, made a doctrine and introduced to the Christian world as an article of faith.

When we ask for the scriptural warrant of this doctrine, we are referred to the writings of St. Paul, especially to the fifth chapter of the Epistle to the Romans. Now, we have the assertion by one of the writers of the New Testament itself that in St. Paul's epistles there are "some things hard to be understood," and when we consider the injurious effects of the doctrine of original sin in the Christian

Church, we are tempted to believe that the writer of Second Peter had this very fifth chapter of the Romans in mind when he added: "which they that are learned and unstable wrest, as they do also the other Scriptures, unto their own destruction." But, whatever be the meaning of St. Paul's speculation about sin and death, we at least have a right to demand that a doctrine of such far-reaching consequence as that of original sin should be borne out by the teaching of Christ himself. And yet, although no one can deny to Christ the keenest appreciation of sin and sinfulness, we search in vain through the gospels for any theory as to the cause of universal guilt. Christ simply recognises the sinfulness of each individual who comes before him, and then he dwells upon and seeks to impress upon men the remedy for sin which he brings.

I believe I am not far wrong in saying that among the theological errors that have caused Christianity to be misunderstood and undervalued, the doctrine of original sin stands in the foremost rank. Its effects upon Christian thought and Christian life have been most injurious. First, it materialises sin. Sin becomes a something outside of ourselves and of everything else; it becomes a thing detached from our inner life. We do not become conscious of it in the affections of our heart, in the processes of our mind; it is a mysterious quantity which is objective to us as anything else outside of us is, with which we therefore deal according to the rules of logical discourse. This materialisation and externalisation of sin inevitably carries with it an impairment of the sense of guilt. This is the most fatal consequence of the doctrine of original sin. It defeats its own purpose. Invented to enhance the importance of sin, its tendency is to do away with the personal sense of sinfulness. For the feeling which the belief in original sin carries with it is something far different from the sense of sinfulness to which Christ appealed and which forms the condition of redemption. When sin becomes a mysterious something, which I am supposed to share with Adam, which is handed down from generation to generation, the sense of guilt is dulled and an æsthetic aversion takes its place. Sin comes to be looked upon as something ugly, revolting; it excites our disgust. The feeling is similar to that caused by a putrifying object or a festering sore. But æsthetic aversion is a very different thing from the consciousness of sinfulness.

It is a necessary consequence of the doctrine of original sin that it weakens responsibility; no amount of reasoning will ever make us feel responsible for Adam's transgression. It also confounds the degrees of sin. Sin conceived as belonging to the race deserves death; there are no degrees of punishment. What is the use of distinguishing degrees of actual sin when I am held to have deserved the extreme penalty for a sin with which I had nothing to do?

It is evident, however, that there is a valuable truth to which the doctrine of original sin gives imperfect expression. Ritschl expresses this truth by means of the phrase: kingdom of sin. That term recognises the fact that sin exists, not as an isolated unconnected fact, but as a complexus of closely related phenomena. It is patent that there are inherited tendencies to sin. I say tendencies, and it is important to mark the distinction. Sin becomes sin only by the actual transgression of the individual will, but there is no doubt that the tendency to transgress may be handed down from father to son. Then there is the propagation of sin by example, the mysterious power by which sin begets sin. These facts make it proper to speak of a law of sin, the law by which, in the complexus of human phenomena, sin is connected with sin. This is the element in the conception of original sin which is founded in fact, but which is better expressed by the term: kingdom of sin.

It is most essential that we clearly realise and firmly grasp this truth: that sin belongs to the individual will. There is no such thing as sin made objective and dissociated from the inner life of the soul. Sin is the peculiar quality of certain acts. Sin no more exists by itself than colour or taste exist by themselves. We speak of blueness, or of bitterness, but no one supposes that these qualities exist apart from the substances to which they belong. So sin does not exist apart from the will or the feeling. Bearing this truth in mind, we now proceed to examine more closely into the nature of sin.

Sin, in the Christian sense, must be understood in relation to the divine will. The Christian assumption is that every human being stands in a certain relation to the divine will. The power over his life has been placed in his own hands, but it is not a matter of indifference to God how he uses that power. A large part of the acts of the individual are indifferent, that is, they have no moral value. They do not determine the quality of his life. But so far as any act determines the value of my life, it is not indifferent to the divine will. God has a purpose with every human being. That purpose is not the same with all, as the parable of the talents shows. Men are variously gifted, and corresponding to his endowments there is an ideal of every man's life. We must suppose that to an omniscient, righteous, loving God this ideal is always present, that he is ever conscious of the purpose of each man's life. Man stands before God, not only as he is, but as he may be. This truth follows from the conception of God as the New Testament gives it to us. From it is deduced a much more comprehensive estimate of sin than that which is commonly held. If there is a divinely recognised purpose to each life, then sin is the deflection from that purpose in the man himself. I make the restriction contained in the last words to guard against any ambiguity from a possible deflection caused from without, by sickness or the action of others, which of course would not be sin. So far then as man by his own action departs from that ideal of his life, which exists in the divine mind, it is sin. God has marked out a certain path for man to travel. Man follows his own inclination and forsakes the path; in so doing he commits sin. Sin is the crossing of the divine purpose.

The most evident manifestations of sin are found in the exercise of the will against the law of God. Sin here is what we call the transgression of God's law. It is a matter of the will. But if the above definition is true, there is also sin of the feeling. It is somewhat difficult to draw the line accurately between will and feeling, but it is of the highest importance to recognise the fact that we sin in our feelings as well as in our will.

In speaking of the feelings, I do not mean such feelings as anger or covetousness, which Christ included under the positive prohibition, nor the ephemeral feelings which come and go; but those fundamental feelings, which go to form what we call our habit of mind, which give quality and direction to our character, which are often unconscious, but which are always there as the substructure of our conscious life: the persistent feelings which make one man differ in disposition from another.

Man is a creature dependent upon God. Do what he will, he cannot get away from that dependence. Now, the question is: What position will he take towards this fact? There is a twofold possibility; he may acknowledge it or he may deny it. If he ignores the alternative, as so many men seem to do, it is equivalent to a denial. But the normal position for man, that which agrees with God's purpose for him, is to acknowledge his dependence upon God. This is the most essential point of difference between men, the acceptance or the denial of dependence upon God. The difference is one of temper, of disposition, of habit of mind. And this temper or disposition or habit of mind is simply that set of feelings, become habitual with us, by which we determine our relation to God. Sin therefore consists as well in aberration of feeling as in aberration of will.

Let me rehearse the salient points of the argument. We have asked, What is sin? In answer we say, Sin is defined as the departure of man, by his own act, from the ideal of his life recognised by God. This departure takes place, first, through acts of the will by active transgressions of the divine law. But we have also found that there may be a departure from the normal life in feeling. This is the religious, as distinguished from the ethical view of sin. It explains to us the fundamental distinction between the God-centred and the self-centred life. The former is normal, the latter is sin.

It now remains to point out in what ways the consequences of sin make themselves felt. In three ways: First, the active transgression manifests itself in the sense of guilt, the accusing conscience. Secondly, sin as wrong feeling makes itself felt in lack of mental peace. The self-centred *mind* does not come to rest. Contrast the serene calm of the Christian mind with the unrest of the mind that has not found God. Thirdly, it is manifest in joylessness. Life's task cannot be done without joy. To the heart alienated from God, life's work is drudgery.

Sin is the negative condition of Christianity. With a deepened sense of sin goes a deeper appreciation of Christianity. A mistake has very commonly been made which has hindered the full Christian appreciation of sin. This consists in measuring sin by the law. The dullness of conscience which the Church has at times manifested, the slowness which she has often shown in recognising a wrong,[1] have been the consequence of that perversion of truth which has made law the ultimate standard. Sin cannot be measured by the law, but only by contrast with goodness. The Christian estimates sin by the standard of the ideal in Christ. Therefore the Christian appreciation of sin is far in advance of the Hebrew or the pagan.

There opens up before us here a subject of extreme interest in the peculiarity of the Christian ideal of life. But I must reserve the consideration of this subject to a future chapter, when I shall speak of the ethical determination of the Christian life. Here I can only point out how by virtue of the infinitely higher ideal of Christianity the appreciation of sin is correspondingly enlarged and deepened. The higher Christian ideal is well illustrated to us in our Communion service. There is first the recitation of the Old Testament Commandments. All but one of these are negative. They tell us what

---

[1] Instance: Slavery and the present corruption in political life.

not to do. Then comes " What our Lord Jesus Christ saith"; and here we have, in contrast to the negative, the positive commandment of love to God and love to man. The ideal which Christ recognised, which we learn from his life and his teaching, is the positive ideal.

This confirms what I said before of the purpose of God with each life. Christ teaches us to recognise the positiveness of that purpose. How infinitely keener and more delicate is the sense of his shortcomings in the man who goes through life with his eye steadily fixed upon an ideal, than his who measures his actions by the dead precept of the law. The law may give you an external, theoretical knowledge of sin, but the subjective inner feeling of sin with which goes the hatred of it, is only possible when one has grasped the ideal of goodness as it has been manifested in Christ.

We started to find the nature of that bar to the state which Jesus called the eternal life, which is the highest conceivable life, the life in communion with God. This brought us to the Christian doctrine of sin. Sin stands in the way of the realisation of that higher life, by alienating man from God and producing within him the feelings of guilt, unrest, and joylessness. It is idle to ask whether sin is a necessity of human nature, whether, theoretically considered, we must not admit the possibility of a sinless development. Whatever may be in theory, practically there is and there can be no life without sin. In the ninth of the Thirty-nine Articles, we read that " Original sin . . . is the fault and corruption of the nature of every man, that naturally is engendered of the offspring of Adam," etc. I do not know that any better account could be given of it than by calling it a " corruption," if we beware of giving a physical interpretation to this term. There is no need of a more exact definition. Sin stands for something radically out of joint in the world. Kant spoke of an " Ur-böse." What that is, no one can tell. All we can say is that it is a necessity laid upon human nature, which acts as a hinderance to its normal development, to the attainment of everlasting life.

We may now proceed to the next stage of our argument.

We have determined two points in life: sin, as man's natural state; the eternal life, as his destined end. What lies between sin and the eternal life? The answer is, Forgiveness. Sin is the obstacle between man and God. It keeps man from God and the eternal life. It must be overcome. Man himself cannot overcome it. God overcomes it, by forgiveness. This is a rough way of stating a very important religious truth. Forgiveness occupies a foremost place as an element of the Christian religion. Christ very clearly recognised this. Instance the story of the paralytic, the sinful woman, the woman taken in adultery, the Lord's prayer: " forgive us our trespasses as we forgive those who trespass against us." The recognition of forgiveness in the words and actions of Christ is too evident that we should fail to recognise it as in his conception a necessary element of the Christian system. To this subject therefore we must give our serious attention.

There is in religion an inveterate tendency to externalisation. Subjective conditions and processes are objectified; they are divested of their ethical character and estimated by quantitative measurement. This tendency is observed in the pagan systems, and it accounts for the constantly recurring superstition in the Christian Church. We found it expressed in the commonly received conceptions of sin. The external *obligatio ad pœnam*, the punishableness, is emphasised as the essential character of sin. Sin and the punishment of sin have been confounded.

Corresponding to this external conception of sin is the idea of forgiveness as the remission or cancelling of punishment. The opinion of mankind has from the beginning coupled moral wrong-doing and physical evil as cause and effect. Suffering is the punishment of sin, and is cancelled by forgiveness. This is a fundamental idea of primitive religion. Homer makes Phœbus send a pestilence into the Greek army in revenge for the insult Agamemnon had offered to the priest Chryses.[1] Nemesis represents the popular belief in the necessary connection between physical punishment and wrong-doing. This doctrine is prominent in the Old Testament. We, however, in the light of the Christ-

[1] *Iliad*. Book I.

ian revelation, are obliged considerably to modify the traditional conceptions. Christ in several cases emphatically denied that guilt was to be inferred from the infliction of suffering. Instance the Galilæans, whose blood Pilate had mingled with their sacrifices, and "those eighteen upon whom the tower of Siloam fell" (St. Luke xiii.). Very striking is the case of the man born blind in St. John ix., where the disciples represent the popular conception of physical evil as the punishment of sin: "Master, who did sin, this man or his parents, that he was born blind?" Jesus unequivocally sets himself against the idea: "Neither hath this man sinned, nor his parents."

Whatever be the organic connection between sin and physical evil—this remains an open question—sin and evil do not necessarily go together as cause and effect in the individual. And therefore the forgiveness of sins cannot mean the cancelling or setting aside of the penalty upon sin in the form of suffering. Christ made the distinction very clear in the case of the paralytic: "Son, thy sins be forgiven thee." And after the assurance of forgiveness, the healing: "Arise, and take up thy bed and go thy way into thine house."

But, it may be said, forgiveness cancels, not present, but future punishment. This relegation to a future time is a convenient disposition of a difficult subject, but it finds no indorsement from the words of Christ. One of the striking peculiarities of Christ's view is a blending of present and future, according to which the characteristics of the life to come are to be found in the life that is.

The association of forgiveness with punishment, as commonly understood, is therefore a habit of mind which must be considerably modified, if we are to understand the function which forgiveness serves in the Christian system. This will be the more clearly apparent if we consider one event in the life of Christ, into which forgiveness enters: the story of the sinful woman with the alabaster box of ointment, in the seventh chapter of St. Luke's Gospel. Jesus declared that her sins are forgiven her. What was the meaning to that woman of Christ's forgiveness? The Pharisee had wondered that he allowed her to touch him, for she was a sinner. He would have no intercourse with her; so far as he was concerned, she was an outcast. But to Jesus she was not an outcast. The heart of the sinning woman had softened. She accepted the divine pardon, and the Son of God received the penitent sinner back into fellowship with goodness and with God. The forgiveness of God was typified in the action of Christ, when in contrast to the Pharisee, who scorned her, he admitted her into human fellowship with himself.

We need but to realise the meaning of forgiveness between man and man in order to understand this. My fellow-man does me a wrong. With that wrong something comes between him and me. Our normal relation of trustful intercourse is marred. The offence he has committed is henceforth a bar to our intimacy. There is an opposition between us. It may not be expressed, but it is felt. The pleasing agreement of will with will, thought with thought, has ceased. There is no longer the old easy, familiar, confident exchange of sentiment. In short, there is a distance between us which had never been before. But now the offence is forgiven; the distance is immediately closed up. It does not mean that punishment is remitted; there is no thought of punishment. But it means the restoration of personal intercourse between man and man; it means the banishment of distrust and suspicion, the resumption of the old intimate understanding. It means that the barrier is removed, and I have taken him once more into the fellowship of my heart. It was this restoration of fellowship with Christ that to the sinning woman constituted her pardon.

Just the same took place with the woman taken in adultery. Although here Jesus does not speak the word forgiveness, it is implied when he says: " Neither do I condemn thee." This story shows us the contrast between the human and the divine way of dealing with men. On the one hand is the law, representing the state with its even-handed justice, demanding death for the adulteress. But there is a greater power than that of the state, the power of divine forgiveness. It did what human justice could not do, it restored the woman to herself and to society.

We found sin to consist in the departure from God's purpose, either in will or in feeling. We can now understand what the punishment for sin really is. It is the feeling of alienation from God. Man is cut off from the source of his life, he becomes a castaway. Like the ship on the trackless ocean whose mariners have been stricken with blindness, so is man without God. This alienation from God is experienced in the form of those feelings which accompany sin: guilt, unrest, joylessness. Forgiveness brings man from alienation to communion. It is the closing up of the breach between God and man. God accepts man into fellowship with himself. Man is placed once more in his normal position. He becomes God-centred. No human language can adequately convey the idea. The relation of spirit to spirit is a mystery which we can but faintly indicate. And yet we understand what is meant.

The heart that finds itself restored to fellowship with God is filled with new feelings. First, there is the peace of conscience. The forgiveness of sins does not mean that all remembrance of sin is cancelled either in the divine or our own mind; but the remembrance of the wrong done is robbed of its sting; it does not prevent the feeling of one-ness in will with God in which the heart comes to rest. There is eliminated the sense of opposition to the will and purpose of God: man has a good conscience.

Then there is the peace of the mind. Says Arthur Hugh Clough in " Dipsychus " :

> " I am rebuked by a sense of the incomplete,
> Of a completion over soon assumed,
> Of adding up too soon."

Many men have felt what the poet felt. A vague feeling of unrest, " a sense of the incomplete," a misgiving that the key to life is wanting, a certain puzzled helplessness in facing life's problem. That insatiable longing of the human mind for a unity of principle in life is not satisfied without God. There is only one point of view from which all the elements of the great world-problem show themselves to us in their true symmetry and proportions, and that is with God. And there is only one way of placing ourselves there, that is through the closing of the chasm between man and God which sin has made: by forgiveness.

Finally, there is the strength for life's work. Man has a task to accomplish, a work to do. We have seen that one effect of sin is a joylessness which clogs all effort. Forgiveness does away with that. No man does successful battle with life unless he is keyed up to that feeling of joy where in the sense of God's continual presence he faces his task with a stout heart. " The fruit of the spirit "—says St. Paul—" is love, *joy*," etc. (Gal. v. 22). It is the privilege of the Christian that he has control of a power before which the dark clouds that had lowered over life's issues and made the event seem uncertain, which have brought despondency to many a heart, are dispelled. To the Christian there can be no such thing as despair. The issues of life he is satisfied to leave in stronger hands; he can look forward serenely to the morrow because he knows that " all things are ours and we are Christ's and

Christ is God's" (1 Cor. iii. 22); his is the privilege which the popular saying describes: One man with God on his side is a majority. This confidence, this courage, this joy comes to him who has been brought into the fellowship with God through forgiveness, which heals the wounds that sin had made.

We have now found the meaning of forgiveness; it is not the remission of punishment in the ordinary sense. It is the bringing back of man to God from the state of alienation in which sin had placed him. But here we meet with a difficulty. Is it not possible that a man might have the same experience as that which has been described as the result of forgiveness, by the reverse process, by the hardening of the heart?

We are puzzled when we find that the peace which we connect with forgiveness is sometimes enjoyed by those who apparently are devoid of religious feelings.[1] There is a large class of people who, without religion, seem to be happy, contented,

[1] The following paragraphs were written under the impression made by large masses of people in great cities. It is this mass of apparently meaningless lives that presents the greatest difficulty to the religious view of life. One cannot at times help feeling as Matthew Arnold did:

> "What is the course of the life
> Of mortal men on the earth?—
> Most men eddy about
> Here and there—eat and drink,
> Chatter and love and hate,
> Gather and squander, are raised
> Aloft, are hurled in the dust,

and peaceful. It seems as if their very stolidity and indifference gave them what religion gives to the Christian. Are we to say that this hardening of the heart, this dulling of the faculties, is a sort of forgiveness? It is this brutish apathy which, more even than the wickedness of life, puzzles and perplexes.

But the question is answered for those upon whom experience has forced it, by another experience—the strongest external evidence, I believe, for Christianity which the execution of the pastoral office furnishes. In the midst of a hopeless dullness and mediocrity of life, from the level plain of stolid indifference, there suddenly flashes upon us a bright example of Christian beauty of life, a life of refinement and acute sensibilities, of deep religious experience and high moral tone.[1] It is such lives as these that show us the difference between confirmed

> Striving blindly, achieving
> Nothing: and then they die—
> Perish:—and no one asks
> Who or what they have been,
> More than he asks what waves,
> In the moonlit solitudes mild
> Of the midmost ocean, have swelled,
> Foamed for a moment, and gone."
>
> *Rugby Chapel.*

And yet one feels rebuked for admitting this view of life to the mind. A truer chord is struck by that other voice that comes down to us through the centuries: "One sparrow shall not fall on the ground without your Father."

[1] One is struck by a refinement of features not infrequently met in such surroundings.

indifference and Christian forgiveness. The fact that such men and women have been enabled to rise above their surroundings gives evidence of the presence of a spiritual power in their lives, and makes us understand that callousness is not forgiveness. It may deaden the heart to the effects of sin, but it leaves the sin itself, the satisfaction with the imperfect life, the brutish complacency in the state of alienation from God.

Forgiveness, bringing man to God, takes away not only the guilt of sin but the sin itself. Not that man becomes sinless; but sin no longer exercises the determination of his life; there is an opposition to sin; the better nature asserts itself against the influences which tend to drag man below the level of man's dignity. This is the secret which so often invests homely lives with a nobility and grandeur, where the peace of life is not the peace of the brute who knows no wants but his appetite, but the peace of manhood, alive to the sense of its worth and its possibilities. This peace belongs to the life of communion with God.

Forgiveness is the process by which that life is entered. It includes therefore two elements: the knowledge of sin and the release from sin.

CHAPTER II.

THE ATONEMENT.

I HAVE used the word "forgiveness" to denote the change that takes place when the sinner is brought from a state of alienation to one of fellowship with God. It is so used by Christ. In the New Testament, however, there are other words which have the same or a cognate meaning. Foremost among them is the word "justification." The prominence which St. Paul gives to this conception is well known. "Justified freely by his grace" (Rom. iii. 24): this was the corner-stone of that grand ideal of the Christian life which has made St. Paul the greatest human exponent of Christianity.

St. Paul had distinct and well-defined conceptions of Christian truth. There are doubtless points at which this conception seems to deflect from that of Christ. But it is no less true that, clothed in a different phraseology, we find largely the same fundamental ideas. We have the idea of the eternal life reproduced. St. Paul does not, it is true, follow Christ in the use of the same words, but speaks out of his own experience. Again, St. Paul's view of the religious determination of that life is equally pronounced. If ever there was a man whose life was determined by his relation to God, it was St. Paul. Finally, what Christ calls " forgiveness," St. Paul called " justification."

The two words stand for the same thing. This has not been generally understood. Forgiveness is supposed to denote a negative operation, justification a positive. It is thought that forgiveness only takes the sin away, but does not impart goodness, that it therefore leaves the sinner in a neutral condition. From this he is translated to a condition of positive value by the process of justification. The fatal objection to this is that it makes forgiveness unintelligible. A process by which the soul remains neutral is inconceivable. As was pointed out in the introduction, we cannot understand anything as affecting the soul except as the effect is manifested in the soul's activity. Forgiveness is unintelligible unless it is evidenced by the active feeling of the soul. It is therefore just as much a positive act as justification. Forgiveness in the language of Christ and justification in the language of St. Paul stand for the process by which the Christian state is entered.

The attempt to differentiate these terms is an instance of how completely the living interests of faith are lost out of sight when logic takes the place of experience. Theologians were even unable to agree as to the order of the two processes, which was to be conceived as first and which as second. As soon as we set aside logical niceties, the matter becomes very simple: Man has not attained, he cannot attain, to his ideal; between him and that ideal there is a barrier. God alone can help him. God does help him. Whether we call it Forgiveness, or Justification, or Adoption, or Reconciliation: all these terms denote one and the same process, the one act of God by which man is brought from a state of alienation to a state of fellowship. The last term, reconciliation, denotes a little more than the others, namely that the process has been brought to completion by man's acceptance of God's gift.

Forgiveness must be understood as an act of God. Here is the point at which the Christian and the naturalisitc conceptions show the most decided divergence. God is not a transcendent, unapproachable being, but one who enters into direct relation with man. This relation is the dominating principle of man's life. Furthermore, it is not merely man who places himself in relation to God, God takes a position towards man. The act by which God forgives man is called by Ritschl an act of " synthetic judgment." The distinction is between this and an " analytic judgment." An analytic judgment is one which is made upon the analysis of the object judged. It is the expression of what actually is. Forgiveness would be an analytic judgment, if it were simply the acknowledgment by God of the state of man such as he finds it. It would then be no more than an expression of a fact. Man is righteous and God by forgiveness declares him to be so. A synthetic judgment comprehends an act of the will by which the object is made to be that which by itself it is not. Man as forgiven by God is something different from that which he was before. And this he is by virtue of the act of God. He owes his new position with whatever that implies to God. He is in the new position through the active exertion of the will of God. Here again, the best guide is the analogy of human forgiveness—Christ placed both on one level when he taught us to pray: "forgive us our trespasses as we forgive those that trespass against us." As with us, when we forgive, there is a positive act of the will, so with God. Forgiveness cannot be reduced to the operation of a natural law. It presupposes a personal divine will.

The idea of forgiveness has become involved in the conception of a judicial process. The first stage of this process is the "satisfaction" of God. After this satisfaction of God's honour or justice has taken place, he pronounces sentence of forgiveness.

This connection between God's forgiveness and his justice owes its origin to the legal ideas which in the Middle Ages obtained a predominant influence in the formation of Christian doctrine. It is a part of that system whose fundamental tenet is the inherent antagonism between God's justice and his mercy. God's anger was turned away by the act of Christ doing satisfaction to the demands of justice. Forgiveness is the sentence by which man is relieved from the penalties of sin. The question is suppressed: What prompted the action of Christ? The theory really attributes to God an attempt at self-deception, making him ascribe that to his justice which had been brought about solely through his mercy.

The consequences of this theory which makes forgiveness part of a judicial process will be developed at another place. Here I wish to call attention to one practical result. In the common mind all that is pleasant and soothing and comforting in religion is connected with Christ, while it contemplates the Father as the stern avenger of wrong. To the majority of Christians probably, God the first person in the Trinity is the God of the Old Testament, or, I should say, of a limited portion of the Old Testament, a denial of the God of the New Testament, while Christ has attracted to himself all the loving features of the God he revealed.

Christ brings forgiveness into relation with God's fatherhood. So in the Lord's Prayer, where the petition for forgiveness is preceded by the invocation of the Father: "Our Father who art in heaven." So too we read: "Forgive . . . that your Father also which is in heaven may forgive you your trespasses"—"But if ye do not forgive, neither will your Father which is in heaven forgive your trespasses" (St. Mark xi. 25 $f.$). In the parable of the prodigal son it is the forgiving father by whom Christ illustrates God's readiness to forgive the penitent sinner. In the high-priestly prayer, in which Christ speaks of his atoning work and of its relation to God, the conception all through is that of the Father. God forgives because he is our Father.

THE ATONEMENT.

In the gospels we find not infrequent expressions of a certain separation which exists between the followers of Christ and others. The peculiar use of the term "world" marks this separation. We read in the high-priestly prayer: " I have manifested thy name unto the men which thou gavest me *out of the world*"—" They are not of the world even as I am not of the world." This idea of separation is carried over into the epistles. St. Paul says: " God hath from the beginning chosen you to salvation " (2 Thess. ii. 13), St. Peter: " Ye are a chosen generation, a royal priesthood, an holy nation, a peculiar people " (1 Pet. ii. 9). When we remember what is so important to bear in mind, that Christ built upon the Old Testament, that therefore the significance of what he did and taught must be learned from the Old Testament, we shall easily find the origin of this conception. It is pointed out by Christ himself at the institution of the last supper: " This is my blood of the covenant " (St. Mark xiv. 24). These words refer to the covenant with Israel (Ex. xxiv. 8). Jeremiah had prophesied a new covenant which God was to make (ch. xxxi. 31). There can be no doubt that Jesus at the institution of the Holy Communion intended to designate himself as the bringer of the new covenant. The old covenant was ratified with the blood of beasts, the new covenant was to be ratified with his own blood. The old covenant was for the forgiveness of sins, the new covenant was a more effective agency for the same purpose. The old covenant was between God and—not the individual Israelites, but Israel as a nation, a community. So, too, the new covenant is between God and—not the individual, but the communion of believers, the followers of Jesus, the Church of Christ, which is chosen out of the world. As we are to understand Christ's intention by reference to the Old Testament polity which to him was the expression of the divine will, we must interpret his purpose of a new covenant as the intended establishment of a corporate body, a new Israel, which was to become heir to the blessings promised to the old Israel, but by them refused. Christ, thinking as a Hebrew, could not have contemplated the individual as primarily the object of his mission. He could not have imagined the Church as a voluntary association of individuals. Such a conception was alien to the idea of a covenant. The covenant could not be with the individual, it must be with the body. Hence, underlying the idea of separation, in the gospels and the epistles, is the opposition to the world of the compact body of believers.

It is necessary to correct the natural bias of our modern ideas, which is strongly individualistic, by reference to the historic genesis of Christian conceptions. We shall be able to express the result as it affects our present conditions in a few words. As seen from the divine point of view, the Church is prior to the individual; it is not the individual believers who by association form the Church, but it is the Church which through the new life that it imparts creates the believer. The meaning of the word as here used is that of the 19th Article: "A congregation of faithful men, in the which the pure word of God is preached," etc. This Church of Christ, or fellowship of believers, is the new Israel which takes the place of the old Israel. It is with this body that the new covenant stands.

It is the Church, therefore, which is primarily the object of the divine forgiveness, and the individual attains that blessing through the Church. It is essential to remember that the Church here does not stand for any order or caste. But even with that reservation, the proposition may seem to involve an intermediary other than Christ between God and man. Christ having once for all opened the way from man to God, it is intolerable to conceive of anything being placed again between us and our creator. But we must not fail to distinguish: it is here not a question of the exercise of the Christian life, but of the genesis of that life. The question is, How does man come into communion with God? and the answer, Through the Church. The Church, as the object of forgiveness, is the sphere within which is realised the blessing which God vouchsafes to man; and it is through the influence of the Church, through training within the Church or through contact with the Church's life, that the blessing is extended to the individual. The Church is the means. It is the organ of forgiveness, it is the body which is opposed to the world as endowed with the power of forgiveness.

There is a sphere of life separated from other life,

which is characterised by its own special traditions, by the exercise of certain functions, and by the common aspiration and the partial attainment of a certian ideal of life. This ideal is not a thing which may be accurately described and communicated in human language. It is something which exists and is perpetuated only in the lives of men. That body or that sphere of common life, which is thus isolated from the general life of the world, is the result of a special relationship entered into by God for the good of mankind. This is the covenant of forgiveness. Forgiveness is the constitutive principle of Christianity as forming the Church. The Church presents that sphere of human society which is determined by the principle of divine forgiveness. The correlate of divine forgiveness is the Church, and the individual so far as he comes within the sphere of the Church. The individual does not make the Church; he always finds the Church present in human society; and so far as he is touched by the peculiar life of the Church, he becomes partaker of forgiveness.

It is an essential requisite of an ethical system that the will of man be conceived as free. This is the advantage of the foregoing theory, that it combines a due regard for God's sovereignty with the preservation of human liberty.[1]

[1] If we conceive God's foreknowledge and forcordination to life to apply, not to the individual, but to the body or fellowship of believers, then the individual's freedom is conserved. God's immutable purpose applies to the Church ; the individual is not predetermined.

The question of the human will has been the most prolific source of theological strife. The refinement of speculative subtlety has drawn the nicest distinctions. The motive of such speculations was the desire of logical precision, which has done so much to turn the minds of men from the true interests of the faith, which has always employed a fruitless metaphysics as the instrument of its investigations, and whose outcome has always been a materialisation of Christianity. We can afford to set aside these subtleties as irrelevant to theology. It is sufficient to know that man's action is simply the acceptance of the divine pardon, the acknowledgement of dependence on God. This is the first step of the Christian life. The fault of the old theology was that owing to its imperfect conception of God too much positive activity was attributed to man in the first act of faith. It was man turning to God. We understand it to be: God seeking man and man accepting God. Man opens himself to God and God enters. The human act is simply one of affirmation.

Here then we have the subjective side of forgiveness. It is expressed in the word "faith." Without faith in man the act of God is incomplete. The justification by which God declares his forgiveness and by which the body of believers, the Church, is drawn from a state of alienation into one of communion with him: that act is perfected in the individual by faith and becomes Reconciliation.

This act of faith is not an act of the intellect. It is not the mere credence given to certain statements of religious truth. In all mental acts every faculty of the mind is employed, and we classify them only according to the prominence of one or the other faculty. There is an intellectual element in faith and an element of feeling; but the predominant factor is the will.

We have to do here with the initial act of faith. It must be carefully distinguished from the mature act. Faith is a growth. We are now considering the inception. We found that forgiveness was the process instituted by God, by which through an act of his will man is brought from sin to eternal life, from alienation to communion. This is the objective act. The subjective correlate is faith, by which man acknowledges his dependence upon the divine will. I need not more than allude to the prominence given to faith in the New Testament. When St. Paul speaks of being "justified by faith," he means that faith is the condition of justification; justification properly is by God alone.

Contrasted with the view of forgiveness here presented, is that which makes law the constitutive principle of Christianity. Man's life is primarily measured by the law. This is the original standard. But man could not keep the law, and forgiveness came in to help him out. At this point there is a diversity of view. On the one hand is the doctrine of man's total depravity. None of his works are good. The law only condemns; hence he is saved by faith and forgiveness. On the other hand, it is held that so far as man keeps the law, he is acceptable to God; forgiveness does away with the effect of inevitable lapses. Law and forgiveness stand side by side.[1]

With this shade of variation, the commonly accepted view of forgiveness assigns to it a secondary, accidental position in the Christian system. The legal relation is first and essential. Forgiveness is somehow adapted to this legal relation. There is no clear differentiation of the distinctively religious from the moral.

Against this view it is maintained, as the fundamental distinction of Christianity, that the one essential, permanent, all-controlling principle of the Christian life is man's spiritual relation to God, of which forgiveness is the expression.

There is a craving in human nature for unity. The mind rests satisfied in the simplicity of one controlling principle. The unity of the Christian life is found in the principle of man's restored fellowship with God, in Forgiveness. One very singular phenomenon connected with Christianity appeals to men with increasing effectiveness in behalf of a gospel of forgiveness: the growth of wickedness along with the growth of goodness. It is prefigured in the story of Christ's life, in the intensifying hatred of the Pharisees and in the hardening of Judas's heart. It is recognised by Christ, where he speaks of the effect of his teaching: "That seeing they may see and not perceive; and hearing they may hear and

[1] Compare the Homily "Of the Salvation of Mankind."

not understand; lest at any time they should be converted and their sins should be forgiven them " (St. Mark iv. 12), and in those words: " Think not that I am come to send peace on earth; I am not come to send peace but a sword " (St. Matt. x. 34), and again in his forecast of the future in the discourse upon the destruction of Jerusalem. It is that fact which has been so puzzling and unaccountable to many, that Christianity seems not only to increase goodness but to increase wickedness. With all the good that Christianity has produced in the world, we stand after eighteen hundred years aghast at the wickedness of man.[1] With all the light of Christianity the dark side of life seems darker than before. Whatever be the explanation—whether the religion which is to restore to man the divine likeness, must of necessity in bringing man to the consciousness of himself and of his power give him the power of evil as well as the power of good, and so bring out all the evil possibilities of his nature as well as the good ; or whether the apparent intensification of sin is more a quickening of the moral sense due to Christianity which makes that appear sin which never was thought sin before—the result is the same: it makes us feel the insufficiency of any merely moral religion and brings home the power of Christianity as the religion of Forgiveness.

[1] This dark side of our Christian civilisation contrasted with heathen virtue, and also its counterpart, the standard of goodness unattained outside of Christianity, is strikingly portrayed by an intelligent Japanese in *The Diary of a Japanese Convert*.

We are now about to take another step forward in our argument. Let us review the salient points of the result we have so far reached. We have established three essential positions. First, the all-important interest of the Christian life is, not conduct but a state; not what we do but what we are—the eternal life. Second, there is an obstacle which prevents man from attaining that life—sin, which rightly understood is alienation from God, either in will or feeling. Third, God does away with this alienation and brings man into fellowship with himself—forgiveness, which is accepted by faith. This forgiveness proceeds from God as Father; it is the constitutive principle of the Christian life, and it belongs to the Church.

The next link in our argument will be that which establishes the connection between Christ and forgiveness. So far we have recognised none. We have left Christ out. Now the question is, What has Christ to do with the religious determination of the Christian life? What is the function of Christ in our life?

Forgiveness, as the constitutive principle of Christianity, is identified with the Church. Where the Church is, there is forgiveness. This fact, in itself, establishes a certain connection between Christ and forgiveness. For Christ was the founder of the Church, and therefore historically the author of forgiveness. We experience communion with God as a privilege common to the fellowship of Christians; to Christ therefore as the founder of that fellowship we trace the forgiveness which brought us into that communion. At the fountain-head of that stream which from its small beginning has grown to be a mighty river, fructifying man's life and clothing it with all the adornments of civilisation, sweet manners, culture, unselfish devotion, heroic endeavour, love of truth and of justice, high aspirations, stands the figure of the Son of man. From him issues the stream of the water of life. The Christian Church with its essential principle of forgiveness marking it off by a distinct line from the world, points ever back to its Founder, to him who came and announced that " The kingdom of God is at hand." In this historic fact of the founding of the Church by Christ we have the connection between him and the principle of forgiveness. He brought it into the world. So far there can be no possibility of doubt. Men in this our day feel themselves brought back from sin and reconciled to God and in that reconcilation they experience a new life, because of what Christ did and said eighteen hundred years ago.

But this places us before a great problem, one which has exercised the powers of the keenest intellects: Did Christ only preach forgiveness? Was it his office simply to declare it as God's messenger? Or, did Christ by what he did effect forgiveness? did he make forgiveness possible? There is this dividing of the ways. There are these two alternatives. The one conception of Christ is that of a prophet, the greatest in a long line of prophets, but still essentially on a level with the ancient prophets. To the belief in Christ as a prophet may be added the attribute of divinity, and yet the conception of his office may remain unchanged; he came to *preach* a higher truth, to announce to man a God who forgives sins. According to this theory it only needed one eminently endowed to bring the truth of forgiveness home to man. Let it be clearly and forcibly presented, as Christ presented it, and man will grasp and cherish it. This is the favourite theory of those who place a great deal of stress upon enlightenment, whose panacea is education. As soon as man knows right —so they reason—he will do right. Christ therefore came to teach, to reveal the truth. His function was to bring a new knowledge.

The fault of this theory is primarily that it undervalues the ethical problem of humanity. Doubtless, enlightenment can do much for humanity. But it must be a broader and deeper enlightenment than that which the mere infusion of knowledge implies. An English teacher has defined education to be " the transmission of life, from the living, through the living, to the living."[1] Taking life in its fullest meaning, no words could more accurately express the law of Christ's work for man. Life is something more than knowledge, it includes the spiritual and the ethical ideal. As such, life can be derived only from the source of all life, Christ. From him it is transmitted, through the living, the Church. Life touching life: this is the idea of Christian edu-

[1] Thring, *Theory and Practice of Teaching*, p. 27.

cation. How meagre, how inadequate, compared with this, is the idea that mere enlightenment, ignoring all the richer part of life, its strong impulses and passions, its moral sense and aspirations, ever had or ever will have the power to regenerate humanity. No more disappointing delusion has ever taken hold of man. The way back from wrong to right, from the sense of guilt to peace of mind, is a more difficult process than the champions of enlightenment fancy, who in a light-hearted way resolve the problem of human sin into the ignorance of childhood which needs only instruction for the human race to outgrow. Such a misconception reveals a total misunderstanding of the nature of those forces that operate most powerfully upon man.

If Christ had been only a prophet and had done no more than preach the truth, he would certainly have failed as every prophet before him failed. But why did Christ not fail? Why is the history of mankind since Christ so vastly different from the history of the centuries before the Christian era? Surely, for no other reason than that in Christ God dealt with the great problem of humanity in a way essentially new, that Christ was something more than a prophet, that he brought to bear upon man's life a motive far more effective than mere knowledge.

Secondly, the language of the New Testament is inconsistent with the prophetical theory of Christ's mission. There are the words of Christ at the institution of the last supper. They might of themselves be interpreted upon the assumption that he was a mere preacher of forgiveness. But when taken in connection with his intention of establishing a new covenant they must mean something more. If Christ made a covenant between God and man, he was more than a mere prophet. Furthermore, this theory offers no explanation of Christ's expressed estimation of himself and his mission. If all Christ did was to declare forgiveness, what will you make of such expressions as: "Come unto me," "I am the good shepherd," "Abide in me," "I am the vine," and many others of like nature? How, finally, according to this theory, shall we understand those words: "The Son of man came to give his life a ransom for many"? Hardly less urgent is the objection from the view which the writers of the epistles held. I need not cite passages to prove that St. Paul believed in Christ as something more than a preacher of forgiveness. It will readily be seen that to reduce gospels and epistles to the level of this theory would amount to such an emasculation of the New Testament as to create as large a problem as had been disposed of.

This brings us to the third objection. To make of Christ a mere prophet is an intolerable offence to the Christian consciousness: and this, by making of Christ himself an unessential element in the Christian system. If Christ only declared God's forgiveness, it is clear that there is a possible Christianity without Christ. One might overleap Christ. When forgiveness has been grasped Christ becomes unnecessary. He is a mere accident in the plan of salvation, Christianity may be conceived with Christ left out. But the heart of Christendom has instinctively clung to Christ as the essential element of Christianity. You cannot conceive of a Christianity without Christ. Any theory which assigns to him a merely accidental position in the Christian scheme has against it the weight of the Christian consciousness of all the ages.

We may therefore consider this conclusion established: Christ is an essential, permanent, necessary factor in the plan of salvation. No theory that ascribes to him a secondary position is true to the facts. Christ is effectively instrumental in bringing forgiveness to man. But here again we are placed before a dilemma: how are we to understand that necessity? is it God's necessity or man's? Was it necessary that Christ should live and suffer because God could not otherwise save man? or because man could not otherwise be saved? We are thus brought face to face with the various theories of the atonement.

It is not my purpose to give an exhaustive survey of the history of this doctrine. There are a few general types around which many variations are grouped, and it will be sufficient to refer to the principal ones of these types. In the Greek Church theological thought was dominated by the idea of the perfection or immortalisation of man through Christ. So far as there was any recognition of a redemption, it was conceived as having been effected by a ransom paid to Satan, namely the ransom of Christ's life. Modifications of this theory long retained their hold in the Christian Church. Traces of it are possibly found in the homily on the Salvation of mankind; although it is not stated directly to whom the ransom was paid.

The theory of the atonement which has taken the strongest hold within the limits of orthodox Christianity is that which bears the name of Anselm. It is called from him because he was the first to gather up the thoughts upon the atonement, which had been floating about, and to combine them into a system.[1] Theological subtlety has been intensely busy, has complicated the doctrine with extensive ramifications, and has produced a bewildering variety of modifications. But the central point, the one essential element of this type, is the thought expressed by the word Satisfaction. God could not forgive man's sin unless his justice or his honour were satisfied, and that satisfaction was made by Christ. That satisfaction may be conceived as having been rendered in several ways, as punishment or as the payment of a debt. Something must be paid for, something must be made up to God; there must be a propitiation, a reconciling of something in God, before he can forgive. God is not

[1] To guard against misunderstanding, I will state that the criticism which follows is directed against the Anselmic doctrine, as it is commonly held and taught to-day. I have no acquaintance with the writings of Anselm, and experience teaches us to guard against a hasty identification of the views of the master with those of his supposed followers.

free of himself to forgive. The field of theology is covered with the remains of systems which have sought to make this assumption plausible. We shall see that, as the theory is commonly understood, it leads to a fatal objection. At this point it is worth while to stop to consider an interesting fact, already referred to, concerning the antecedents of this doctrine.

There had been in the Latin Church from the beginning a tendency to a legal view of religion. The genius for the law which had characterised the Roman State was received as an inheritance by the Latin Church. To the converted barbarian nations the Church was represented largely as a system of legal enactments. The Gospel as a "glad news" became obliterated, the sum of religion was what man *must* do, what he *must* believe, what he *must* pay. The tendency was to draw more and more of Christianity within the scope of the law. Finally, the great doctrines themselves yielded to this tendency, and came to be judicially interpreted. In the course of time legal phrases and their corresponding conceptions had made themselves at home in theological phraseology, such as Judge, Indictment, Satisfaction, Penalty.

The use of terms in analogy is very insidious and apt to be misleading. In the sphere of religion, where we are dealing with spiritual things, we make very large use of this form of speech; all the greater should be our care to see that the analogy is justified. For after the term which we have borrowed from another sphere has been used for a sufficient length of time, it comes to be considered as having a native right in its new surroundings and we are apt to forget that it is borrowed. So it has been with the legal phrases used in religion. Their origin has been lost sight of. The relation suggested by the Anselmic theory of the atonement between God and man has been unreservedly accepted. The fact seems to have been lost sight of, that the use of legal terms and the conceptions of legal processes in religion are merely the application to the spiritual and heavenly of terms and forms borrowed from one circumscribed sphere of human life. The world of thought in which the Christian mind to-day largely moves is the world of law. One narrow sphere of human interests is expanded so as to bring under the sway of its ruling principles all the fundamental conceptions affecting the eternal well-being of man. This view makes the kingdom of God a huge Roman empire. The question is, whether this analogy is justified.

The third type of doctrine of the atonement is that of Abelard. The fundamental conception underlying Abelard's theory is that of God's love. Christ in his life and his death is the expression of God's love. There was no reconciliation necessary between the demands of justice and those of love. Christ did not propitiate the wrath of God. Whatever God's justice is, it is subordinate to his love. The manifestation of God's love in the life and death of Christ was given in order to awaken man's love of God. God might have forgiven sins without Christ, but Christ was necessary to induce man to confide in God. Other elements are attached to this theory: the recognition of Christ as the head of humanity whose merits are imputed to man, and the conception of Christ's continued intercession for us in heaven. But the essential feature is the conception of the life and death of Christ as being the expression of God's love for man to awaken his love.

Of these three theories, thus briefly outlined, we may leave out of view the first. It belongs entirely to the past. The other two, those named after Anselm and Abelard, may be taken as the opposite poles towards which all modifications of the doctrine of the atonement tend to approximate. They agree in making Christ an essential element in the Christian system, but they differ in that the first makes Christ necessary on God's account, the second on account of man.

The first represents the most widely accepted view. It is the view which is generally considered as underlying all "personal religion." This implies a keen sense of sin, the consciousness of God's wrath resting upon me as a sinner, the impossibilty of my appeasing that wrath, the joyful acceptance of the assurance that Christ has borne my sins and saved me from God's wrath. It is commonly supposed impossible to bring the sense of forgiveness home to the sinner unless he is assured that the punishment which he should bear, is borne by another.

This means that the sinner will not believe in forgiveness unless he understands just how God forgives. But the sinner who has so much theological curiosity may ask further: If Christ induced an angry God to forgive sins, who induced God to send Christ ? In fact, the practical necessity of this view is an unwarranted assumption. Christ has perhaps been presented to the sinner most frequently with this view of the meaning of his life and death accompanying the presentation. But that does not prove that there is not a power in Christ's life and death to bring assurance of forgiveness without this theory.[1]

On the other hand, there can be no doubt that the doctrine of the atonement, according to this theory, has been and is still a great stumbling-block. If it were this in the sense in which, according to St. Paul, the gospel was a stumbling-block to the Jews, this would be no objection. But it is a stumbling-block, not so much to the worldly as to sin-

[1] I have, since writing the above, again read Lyttleton's essay on the Atonement in *Lux Mundi*. One is strongly impressed with the noble tone of this as of the other writings in that volume. But I was also impressed with the artificiality of the doctrine as there presented. After all, the crux of the question lies in the assertion, strongly insisted upon by Mr. Lyttleton, of the practical and spiritual necessity of a propitiation. If the belief in the propitiatory value of the death of Christ is an essential condition of our religious life, it is a " mystery," which we have to acknowledge, although we cannot explain it. I cannot accept this view. Compare on the other hand William Law's essay on the Atonement. Law was the author of the *Serious Call to a Devout and Holy Life*, which strongly influenced John Wesley and which made an epoch in the life of Doctor Johnson.

cere seekers for truth, to men who are longing for an adequate satisfaction for their religious wants, but do not find it in a doctrine which puts insuperable difficulties in the path of honest thought.

What are these difficulties? We have seen that the essential point of this doctrine as commonly held is the conception of a necessary satisfaction of God's justice. The difficulty comes when you pursue this thought to its consequences in the nature of God. Here is the touchstone for all theological theories: What effect have they upon our conception of God? Is God, under this theory, thinkable or not? The consideration of this point is reserved for another chapter, when I shall speak of the idea of God. I shall here only anticipate the conclusion, that the Anselmic theory involves the idea of God in a fatal contradiction. It sets God against himself and makes it impossible to think God. It is therefore opposed to our religious interests, and, whatever its pedigree and prestige, it must be rejected. It is not in the appeasing of an angry God that we find the necessity under which Christ became man, suffered and died.

The solution of the problem must be sought along the lines marked out by Abelard. The life and death of Christ were necessary on account of man. Here we start with God's forgiveness as a fact. God has pardoned man's sin, God is ready to receive man back into communion with himself. But God does not force man into communion. Man is free to accept or refuse. Christ was necessary to induce man to turn to God and accept forgiveness. To bring man to God, not God to man, was the " work " which the Father had given him to finish (St. John iv. 34). For this he instituted the new covenant and sealed it with his blood " for the forgiveness of sins." For this he gave his life a " ransom (price) for many " (St. Mark x. 45). He lived in perfect communion with the Father and to bring his disciples to the same communion was his object: " Father, I will that they also whom thou hast given me be with me where I am " (St. John xvii. 24).

To a superficial way of thinking it is unintelligible that to bring forgiveness home to man should cost so much. Forgiveness seems so natural. But they who reason thus forget that the very naturalness of forgiveness is owing to the Christian surroundings in which they have been brought up. They are like people in a house, who feel how firm and solid the house stands and wonder why the architect found it necessary to build such strong foundations when it stood so firm. It is difficult for us, brought up as we are from infancy with Christian ways of looking at things, surrounded on all sides by Christian influences, to realise how great is the difference Christianity has made in the world. The introduction of the Christian religion was the raising of mankind to a new level. And to the magnitude of the effect corresponded the magnitude of the cause.

It requires something more than the knowledge of the forces which operate on the surface of life to understand man's true position in the universe, to see clearly the steps in the orderly progress of humanity to higher levels of civilisation, and to forecast the future destinies of the race: for this is needed an adequate knowledge and appreciation of ideal forces.

The gradual elevation of man presents to the student of history the spectacle of a process immeasurably laborious. Step by step has the advance been made, and every step forward has been won by a long struggle. Whatever was true in the earlier ages of the world, when man had not so far distanced the rest of creation, when as yet he remained but half-conscious of himself, of our own age we may confidently say, that no such forward movement could take place unless there were a mighty spiritual propelling motive. And when we ask, What is this propelling motive? we are led to contemplate the ideal forces which are working in men's lives, and these forces we find focused in one point, the atoning work of Christ upon earth.

This may serve to mark the outlines of our problem. We see in the Church of God many influences at work; each of these may be considered apart, separate, isolated from its connexions and antecedents. But a deeper insight will trace these influences to the one central fundamental force, the power of Christ's atoning work. " I, if I be lifted up from the earth, will draw all men unto me ": this was Christ's prophecy. He told of the Spirit who should come to take his place. The forces which work for Christ are spiritual forces, and whoever has eyes to see can recognise, under the surface of history, underlying the obvious phenomena of progress, the working of these great spiritual forces. But behind these spiritual forces, at the point from which they all radiate, stands the figure of the historic Christ, the story of his life.

The Church carries out the work of Christ. The power working for Christ in the Church is the power of personal life, by its nobility and sweetness drawing men to the knowledge of Christ; or the life of the Church as a body, by its Christian activity or through the highest expression of its life, in its worship, continuing Christ's influence upon earth. It is life touching life, "from the living, *through the living*, to the living," and wherever through the influence of living man there is kindled a higher sense of human possibilities as they are manifested in the life of the God-man, there Christ is active. Christ works through the lives of living men. This is the great truth of the Church. She represents the sphere of forgiveness, the principle of the higher life, because in her has always dwelt some of the power of Christ. From generation to generation she has passed on the power and the knowledge of Christ. Oftentimes has tradition distorted the features in the picture which she handed down; but never so that some of the truth of Christ's life was not carried with it and some of the power of Christ was not present, either in the worship and the ministrations of the Church or in the lives of those who were Christ's. So Christ works in the present through the spiritual powers in his Church. There is no thought which gives such high dignity to human life and lays upon us such weight of responsiblity as this.

But wherever there is the power of Christ in human life it rests upon the historic Christ; and therefore I said that the manifestations of the Spirit's power centre in the life of Christ. That power is like a stream. Men come to drink of it far down in the valley; but the water issues from the ground high up in the hills. All power comes ultimately from the life of Christ. That life is God's mighty argument with men. There is no magic influence going out from Christ to save man. The power of Christ is the power of his earthly life, to bring home to man the sense of God's forgiveness. A man may be roused to an appreciation of himself, of his needs and his possibilities, by the influence of a life of Christian devotion in some fellow-man. But the impression will be fleeting unless he goes to the fountain-head of power: the life of Christ. God, as we believe, has preserved for us the record of that life, and it is through the knowledge which we may have from the gospels of the inner life of Jesus that he chiefly exerts his saving power. The wonderful power of the story of Christ's life has always been felt. Says Leopold Ranke: " Even from the worldly point of view whence we consider it, we may safely assert, that nothing more guileless or impressive, more exalted or more holy, has ever been seen on earth than were his life, his whole conversation, and his death. In his every word there breathes the pure spirit of God. They are words, as St. Peter has expressed it, of eternal life. The records of humanity present nothing that can be compared, however remotely, with the life of Jesus." These are the words of the dispassionate historian.[1] This is the impression which his keen, comprehensive mind received from the life of Jesus. But it requires no keenness of intellect to appreciate the beauty of that life. The inner life of Jesus discloses itself in some measure to all who seek to make it their own. That means something more than a mere intellectual appreciation of Christ's life. It implies the sympathetic spiritual appropriation of the Son of God.

The influence of that life, as it enters more and more into the consciousness, will be twofold. First,— it convinces of sin. Though the moral sense may slumber in many, there is no man without it, and there can be no way of rousing that moral sense more effective than placing before the mind the beauty of that one life and its sufferings in behalf of man.

Christ brings sin home to man, and so he answers one great need of humanity. Without the consciousness of sin there can be no forgiveness, no peace. Those who live sunk in sin and brutishness, whatever hope there is for them, it is not from the law. The law may inspire fear, but will not bring to God. Our trust is in the influence of Jesus, that

---

[1] *History of the Popes*, Book I. chap. i. § 1.

a knowledge of the one perfect life will stir the dormant aspirations for something better and awaken a consciousness of their own wants.

And then Jesus brings home the assurance of forgiveness. At the other extreme from moral indifference is moral sensitiveness. Many are so keenly alive to the greatness of sin that they can hardly believe in a possible forgiveness. The more we learn of life, the darker grows the picture. The consciousness of human sin has weighed heavily upon the heart of Christendom. But the very weight of the sin makes the feeling of relief all the greater which the gospel of forgiveness brings.

Just here we see the marvel of the atonement. It is the meeting of the greatest sin with the greatest love. What is the sin of our time to the sin done against Jesus? to the hatred and cruelty inflicted upon him who gave his life for man? The antagonism of wickedness to goodness reached a climax in the life of Jesus. And yet, in spite of it all, we see in him an unbroken, unfaltering, trust in God's purpose to carry to a successful issue the intent of his mission and a steady perseverance in his work of mercy. Christ might be stirred to burning indignation against the hypocrisy of the Pharisees, the sight of Jerusalem might fill his soul with keen disappointment, such as found expression in his memorable lament; but neither the opposition of his enemies nor the sense of present failure could make him waver one instant in his faith, that his life was to be for the healing of the nations, or turn him aside from the loving service which made up his life's work. It is only when we view this persistence of Christ against the background of man's wickedness, as it arrayed itself against him, that we are able to measure in any sense the significance of his atoning work. Is there anything more sublime or powerful than that calm assurance in the face of a cruel death: " Peace I leave with you, my peace I give unto you " ? Surely there could be no more convincing proof of God's forgiving love to man than the life of Christ.

This then is the twofold effect of Christ's atoning work. It rouses the indifferent to a sense of sin, and him who is tempted to despair of man it assures of the divine forgiveness. But here we may be met with this question: Does not this, after all, conceive of forgiveness as something apart from Christ ? Does it not really make Christ unnecessary ? Is it not possible, with this view, to have fellowship with God without Christ ? Theoretically, yes. We may conceive of God as revealing himself to man directly, so that he enters into fellowship with him without the intervention of Christ. But with the conditions such as they are, Christ is a necessity to Christian faith. There may be, there doubtless is, a faith in God without Christ; but such faith is an imperfect faith. It is a faith to which a man has no right, because he cannot give account of it; such a faith is dangerous. They say a man may walk over the most dangerous places asleep, but let him wake up and he is lost. So it is with those men who have faith without Christ. The faith which is without the consciousness of the only valid ground of faith is the faith of sleep. The danger is that some sharp stroke of fortune or some before unheard-of difficulty will suddenly awaken the man, and then he is lost.

This is what we have got to come back to: Christ is the only ground we have of believing in a merciful God who forgives sin; and we would not believe this truth, which almost daily experience seems to belie, if Christ had not brought it home to us in the most convincing manner. And so we believe that God has in his infinite wisdom appointed Christ as the means whereby man is to be saved. We believe that we are to learn to believe in God by believing in Christ. We believe that God's forgiveness embraces those who shall become followers of Christ, his Church. We believe that the Church is the divinely appointed means for bringing to man the benefits of Christ. We believe therefore that God wills that we should receive forgiveness by entering into the fellowship of Christ's Church. These appear to us elements of that device by which God in his love seeks to save man. Farther than that we cannot go. We dare not draw the limits of God's mercy and say that if some man, neglecting the divinely appointed means, the Church and Christ, seeks God, God will refuse him. Enough, that we know what the way is *for us*.

It is, however, important to point out that Christ is the means to the end. Christ pointed away from himself to the Father. There is a certain type of faith which does not get beyond Christ. In so far as it fails to reach God through Christ, it fails of the standard set by Christ. Especially is that form of Christianity which rests in the contemplation of Christ's sufferings a gross deviation from Christian truth. Christ's sufferings bring home to us the depth of human sin, but the brooding contemplation of his sufferings substitutes an æsthetic feeling for faith and is a sensualisation of Christianity. We believe in Christ because in him we find God.

The place here assigned to Christ in the Christian system is irreconcilable with that modification of Christian theory which is widely prevalent to-day, especially among those who turn aside in impatience from what seems to them an idle strife of tongues, the wrangling about doctrine. They seek refuge in the simplicity of that Christianity which sums up the Christian truth in the one word: imitation of Christ. It is a relief to cast off all subtleties and to rest in one easily understood principle. One of the latest exponents of modern Christianity tells us that this, after all, is the great thing. "Jesus," says Mr. Gordon, "is our supreme example. There is in him a mighty, imitable, reproducible character. The imitation of Christ is the task of humanity."[1] We cannot but rejoice that different men may find different points of attraction in Christ. But the deeper consciousness of Christendom refuses in the

[1] George A. Gordon, *The Christ of To-day*, p. 67.

nineteenth century, as it always has refused, to content itself with this apparent simplicity and to recognise therein the essential element of Christianity. A little reflection will serve to show how inadequate this expression is. Imitation is of the outward: you can imitate a man's dress, his house, his voice, etc. In this way imitation comes prominently into play in childhood. The child learns its first lessons by imitating the actions which it observes in older people. But imitation in spiritual things is of very limited application. We may occasionally correct our judgment by reference to the example of Christ. But how little adapted this principle is to become the regulative principle of the Christian life, we will understand when we try to conceive of a character formed by imitation upon some other human character. Conceive of a Cromwell or a Washington as great because they *imitated* somebody. Attempts at imitation, as is well known, make a person not great or good, but ridiculous. There is that in the conception of human character which is incompatible with imitation. This is the secret of character which finds its only explanation in man's relation to God. If we honestly seek to make ourselves as Christ was we shall not try to piece together a patchwork of character after his model, but we shall strive to appropriate the fundamental principle of his life.

The idea of the imitation of Christ is furthermore unfortunate, because it places us on a level with him. To say that Christ is an " imitable, reproducible character " may be from one point of view an innocent assertion. There are doubtless moments in life when Christ appears as one of us, fighting the same battle of life. But such language is wholly misleading if it would point out what should be the Christian's fundamental attitude. Christ claimed to be unique; his significance to the world is that he is unique, inimitable, not reproducible. If it were otherwise, Christianity would never have been what it has been these eighteen centuries. To place Christ on a level with humanity is altogether to miss the personal and the historic significance of his life. It is robbing Christianity of its religious character, to make it a morality.

Christ stands out from all history as the one human character in whom God made himself known to man, that by him man might be brought, through forgiveness, into fellowship with God.

CHAPTER III.

THE ETERNAL LIFE.

WE have traced the various elements that enter into the consideration of the Christian life as religiously determined. The object of Christianity is to realise the eternal life. Sin is the barrier to the enjoyment of that life. God's act of forgiveness is necessary to do away with the effects of sin; this act is therefore the constitutive principle of the Christian life. Forgiveness is bound up with Christ; through him alone we are brought into fellowship with God.

The subjective manifestation of forgiveness or justification is faith. In its incipient stage that faith is simply the acceptance of God's gift. But it is a growing faith. There is a beginning of the Christian life and a progress. What was at first merely an act of spiritual affirmation becomes enlarged, deepened, enriched. Faith develops into trust, it becomes more and more the dominating principle of life, it matures into the conscious love of God. With this growing faith there goes hand in hand the ethical determination of life to make the perfect Christian. But the religious is fundamental; it is the essential determination of the Christian life.

Before there can be any true ethical life the soul must have found its true relation to God.

We will now consider somewhat more fully this "eternal life" into which the Christian enters through Christ. In that life we have come into a living fellowship with God; a new principle asserts its power over us; an influence has been awakened; we have passed into the spiritual life, in which there is a communication of spiritual forces. We recognise in the eternal life a direct relationship to God, a communion or communication between God and man which is realised in prayer.[1] This is the peculiarity of the God-centred life, that it looks away from self to God. All is traced to God. God, not ourselves, is the author of the new life, the principle of growth within us: "It is God which worketh in you both to will and to do of his good pleasure" (Phil. ii. 13).

Here we stop to notice a striking contrast between character as formed on worldly principles and Christian character. The former is a finality, to the Christian there can be no finality of character. The

[1] Ritschl's treatment of the Christian's personal relation to God, and of prayer, is obscure and unsatisfactory. One reads and re-reads passages bearing upon this question without being able to get at the exact meaning. He denies the possibility of an immediate, direct, spiritual relationship, and yet one has a lurking suspicion that in a way peculiarly his own he allows it. The same is true of one of Ritschl's most eminent pupils, Herrmann, in his *Verkehr des Christen mit Gott*. I thought I understood the meaning of the word "Verkehr," communion. But after a careful perusal of this volume I was sure I did not understand it, at least in the sense in which the author uses the word.

common estimation identifies strength of character with persistency and unchangeableness. It is the crystal, clear-cut, sharply defined, unyielding. Such have been many who have powerfully influenced their fellow-men, men of great force. Christian character has nothing of the same crystalline immutability, and therefore it is by the undiscerning mistaken for weakness. Because it is God-centred, not self-centred, it is not so imposing; there is an absence of the self-assertion and the show of confidence, which have always won the plaudits of the multitude. But its strength is of a finer quality and more enduring. It is the strength of an Athanasius, who with God on his side is equal to the world. Christian character, so far from being immutable, is ever growing. With every increase of light it takes to itself new strength and new beauty. So far from fearing change, it fears to get beyond change. For change means growth, increase, progress. The thing the Christian dreads most is the possibility of that rigidity coming over him, which the world takes for strength, but which to him is weakness. For he is not sufficient unto himself; his strength is God's, he looks above for all he needs, and he hopes it will come to him more and more.[1]

In the introductory chapter it was pointed out that a true theory of psychology demands that we trace every influence upon the soul in the active

[1] It is interesting to trace in art the difference between the two types of character. Compare a Venus of Milo with a Sistine Madonna, or the illustrations of DuMaurier with the paintings of Fra Angelico.

feelings. We may not deal with the soul as if it were a something behind those feelings in which it manifests its activity. We cannot separate the active functions of the soul, its will, feeling, and knowing, from the soul itself, and treat the latter as a passive quantity. We cannot say that the soul is "saved," "forgiven," "justified," "brought to God," unless that salvation, forgiveness, justification, or approach to God expresses itself in the soul's activity by certain feelings. Therefore we shall have to trace that state of the Christian which Christ called the "eternal life" by its manifestations in the new feelings awakened in the soul when it is brought to God.

What is the scope of the feelings which are thus brought into activity? The question has very great significance. To put it somewhat differently, What relationships in life are affected by religion? What life is it, or what part of life, that is determined by religion? Schleiermacher maintained that religion consisted in the feeling of dependence upon God. This view would confine the religious determination of life to our relation to God. It is our feelings towards God that religion regulates. But from the words of Christ we seem to get a hint of a larger conception: " In the world ye shall have tribulation: but be of good cheer; I have overcome the world " (St. John xvi. 33). By the word "world," which he says he has overcome, Christ means that complexus of forces, partly physical partly personal, with which every being comes more or less in contact, which oppose themselves to the aims of the individual: sickness, death, disappointments, injustice, ill-will of fellow-men, etc.

It is impossible to leave "the world," as so understood, out in the consideration of religion. It is impossible to understand the dependence upon God except as carrying with it the independence of the world. Man's religious life must be considered not only as a relation to God, but also as a relation to the world. In these two relationships, in the feelings which belong to them, we shall trace the manifestation of the " eternal life." As far as man enters into an eternal life, he must feel himself in a new position, not only in regard to God, but also in regard to the world. The *faith in God's providence* combines the feeling of dependence upon God with that which should characterise the Christian's relation to the world. It is the feeling that the God whom we trust will so guard us that the world cannot hurt us. This is the faith in God as Christ understood it.

It is a shortcoming of our modern theology that it fails of a correct appreciation of this faith in God. And yet it was an essential element in Christianity to the first Christians; for nothing is so marked as the emphasis with which this faith, as expressive of the superiority to the world, is stamped upon the epistles of the New Testament. St. Paul speaks of " the liberty wherewith Christ hath made us free " (Gal. v. 1). He can mean nothing but liberty from the world, understood as the complexus of forces which oppose themselves to man's pursuit of his end. St. Paul points to a well-known experience. The " natural man " is dependent upon the powers of nature and the will of his fellow-men; they impress themselves upon him as superior, his will cannot obtain the mastery. He is a slave. And when St. Paul says that Christ has set him free, he but experiences the fulfilment of the promise: " Ye shall know the truth and the truth shall make you free " (St. John viii. 32). It is the paradox of the Christian life, that without any change of outward relation there is a reversal of feeling,—a process beyond explanation upon a naturalistic hypothesis, yet there is none that experience teaches as so true. The bonds are broken, the feeling of dependence upon the world is changed into one of freedom. What was before a hindrance to our free action becomes an aid to the completer development of our individuality.

The expression of St. Paul just quoted receives its commentary in those glorious words of his in the eighth chapter of Romans: " If God be for us, who can be against us ? . . . Who shall separate us from the love of Christ? Shall tribulation, or distress, or persecution, or famine, or nakedness, or peril, or sword ? . . . In all these things we are more than conquerors through him that loved us. For I am persuaded, that neither death, nor life, nor angels, nor principalities, nor powers, nor things present, nor things to come, nor height, nor depth, nor any other creature, shall be able to separate us from the love of God, which is in Christ Jesus our Lord." And that same sense of superiority to the world is in those other words, in the third chapter of the First Corinthians: "Therefore let no man glory in men. For all things are yours; whether Paul, or Apollos, or Cephas, or the world, or life, or death, or things present, or things to come; all are yours; and ye are Christ's; and Christ is God's." St. Paul speaks elsewhere of reigning through Christ: "They which receive abundance of grace and of the gift of righteousness shall reign in life by one, Jesus Christ." The expression here as elsewhere [1] is the Greek verb βασιλεύειν; the idea is that of kingship. The Christian is a king; the Christian faith gives him dominion of the world. He now rules those forces which before had ruled him. This, not in the sense that they no longer affect him outwardly, but that his inner life is untouched by them. He is above them: "From henceforth let no man trouble me; for I bear in my body the marks of the Lord Jesus." The disappointments the great apostle had suffered in his efforts for Christ would have embittered most men. He simply falls back upon his own individuality as it is fixed in Christ. Whatever others do does not trouble him; in the sacred sphere of his own personality he is above it all.

[1] Rom. v. 17; cmp. 1 Cor. iv. 8. How little the Pauline idea of "reigning," of the superiority to the world, has been understood, is curiously illustrated in one of our prayers. In the Collect for Peace in the Morning Prayer, the sentence, "Whose service is perfect freedom," is a modification of the original, which in the Sarum Breviary reads, "cui servire regnare est."

The world-conquering character of the Christian faith finds striking expression in the often-repeated promises in the Revelation to those who " overcome," as, to take one verse out of many, in chapter iii. 5: " He that overcometh, the same shall be clothed in white raiment; and I will not blot out his name out of the book of life, but I will confess his name before my Father and before his angels." The same thought is echoed in the Epistles of St. John (I. ch. v. 5): " Who is he that overcometh the world, but he that believeth that Jesus is the Son of God." The idea is identical with that expressed by St. Paul under the name of Christian liberty. We find it again in St. Peter's Epistle. Here it appears as the joy, which is the expression of the Christian's superiority to the world: " Rejoice, inasmuch as ye are partakers of Christ's sufferings; that, when his glory shall be revealed, ye may be glad also with exceeding joy " (I. ch. iv. 13). The same in St. James (ch. i. 9): " Let the brother of low degree rejoice in that he is exalted." In this Epistle we meet again with the idea of Christian liberty, when St. James speaks of " the perfect law of liberty " (ch: i. 25).

But it is not so much in special expressions that this mark of Christianity is to be sought for in the New Testament, as in the general tone, in the underlying feeling. For this sense of dependence upon God and trust in divine providence exists not always in a conscious mental act; faith is not always present to the mind in the shape of a distinct proposition. We possess it mostly as a sort of temper, a disposition of heart and mind, an underlying ground-tone which gives quality to our spiritual life. It is this ground-tone, this underswell of faith in God as against the world, that runs through the epistles of the New Testament, and more than anything else gives them their distinctive character.

This faith in God differentiates the Christian spirit from what is commonly known as optimism. The latter is a haphazard quality. Take two men, one an optimist, the other a pessimist. They look at things differently. Why? Probably for one or both of two reasons: for the personal experience which has differently affected each, or for differences of temper and disposition owing to physiological causes. Optimism, as commonly understood, has no other foundation than these two: it is either the result of a fortunate experience, or it is owing to a happy disposition or good circulation and digestion. Christian optimism has nothing to do with these things. It believes in the world because it believes in God. It makes no difference what may happen; to the serene confidence of the Christian the ultimate victory of the good is secure. Christian optimism has a very wide outlook; it is ready for many disappointments, it counts only upon ultimate triumph. It has a very broad field; it cannot embrace less than humanity; it dare not bind itself to one nation or race. No amount of Christian optimism would have saved the Roman empire; Christian optimism cannot to-day rest secure in the belief that God will save the American people, if they defy the eternal laws of right and truth.

Christian faith is something different from stoical resignation. The latter is passive; it lets the waves of adversity roll over it without opposition or murmur. The spirit of Christianity is an active spirit. It is that feeling of superiority which is not content to yield to the forces of the world, but cherishes an active principle of opposition. It is not a numbing of the powers and feelings of the individual, it is the most pronounced assertion of the rights of individuality. It is the courage of the man, not the indifference of the brute. So far from being identical with mere endurance, the Christian faith is full of joy. It faces life's tasks with that elated feeling of mastership that comes alone with the conviction that a power higher and stronger than ourselves is on our side, that "all things work together for good to them that love God." With that courage for the struggle goes the mental peace. We found, when we spoke of sin, that the state of separation from God is characterised not only by an accusing conscience and the sense of guilt, but also by a mental unrest and discontent. It is the feeling of helplessness and bewilderment of the godless life. Life without God is an enigma, a confused mass of conflicting phenomena. It is for the want of the key to life, which is in God alone, that the lives of many seem like one prolonged labour of

Sisyphus, a straining after a satisfaction which is never attained.

What is more striking in the life of Jesus than its perfect calm? It is this which carries with it so impressively the suggestion of strength. When we think of the feelings within his breast, how tumultuous at times they must have been; the indignation at wrong-doing, the impatience with narrowness, the shock to his patriotism, the pain at his countrymen's ingratitude, the bitterness of failure, the wounding of his tenderest sensibilities, the disappointments over the weakness and slow comprehension of his disciples, and finally the physical suffering—how wonderful is not the even, unbroken calmness of his life! Through it all, perfect self-possession, a heart and mind at peace, no trace of discord in the inner life, no bewilderment or wonder at the strangeness of his lot, no complaint, no impatience—just a calm, self-collected, God-centred strength. We shall always have to go back to the life of Jesus, not to find a model to copy, but an ideal of Christian character, which shows us what man may become.

It is this God-centred strength that forms the chief element of Christian character. You may call it by many different names, the liberty of the Christian, independence, the dominion over the world, or simply faith; it is that quality which has translated itself into our modern vocabulary in the use of the word character. It is the same as that which Christ calls the eternal life. It is the "life hid with Christ in God," the outcome of that forgiveness which brings man back from a state of alienation to God, to the source and sustainer of his being, and places him there in his true abiding-place, that on that vantage-ground, at the centre and fountain-head of all being, he may experience what else were impossible, the value of his own soul and its superiority as against the world. And in this new position the Christian enjoys assurance of salvation. He is saved, in the present and for all coming time.¹

In his essay on Carlyle's *Cromwell*, Mr. Mozley has a fine description of the poetical type of the hero. "A hero," he says, "is a person, who in some special and marked way, shows, under a surface of outward activity and adventure,—that of the military life especially,—a soul superior to and not belonging to this world." The appellation is confined to the few who, either in ancient or in Christian times, have been exhibited to us as possessing those qualities under peculiar and distinguishing circumstances. But Christianity has really made heroism the common property of all. It is no longer the distinguishing characteristic of a few who have drawn the world's gaze upon themselves. Heroism is of the very essence of Christianity, and it is im-

¹ It is at this point that the practical difference between the Roman and the Evangelical systems is especially apparent. One of the chapters of the Decrees of the Council of Trent is directed "Contra inanem hereticorum fiduciam," and closes with these words: "Cum nullus scire valeat certitudine fidei, cui non potest subesse falsum, se gratiam Dei esse consecutum." It has been well said, and the saying admirably characterises the two ideals of religion, that the end of the Roman system is to be safe, that of the Protestant to be sure.

possible to draw the line at any particular degree of glamour and brilliancy which must surround the man to make him a hero. There is no generic difference between the heroism of a rock-chained Prometheus and that of the poor seamstress in the back alley working her fingers to the bone to support an aged mother, uncomplaining, sustained in her brave struggle by a Christian faith. Christian heroism is simply superiority to the world exhibiting itself under adverse circumstances.

Our popular religion is much at fault in leaving out of consideration this relationship of Christianity to the world. It has largely failed to comprehend that this faith in God as against the world is the true and proper goal of Christian aspiration, constitutes the Christian life. There has been always a tendency to seek for a higher, more distinctive, meaning in the Christian life. This trust in God's providence was too simple, it became associated with "natural religion," and its connexion with Christianity was lost sight of. Something above and beyond it, something peculiarly and essentially Christian, was demanded.

Mysticism claims to be a higher type of Christianity. Not that there is not something mysterious and mystical in that faith whose essential nature is communion with God; but mysticism proper is something beyond this. As a movement of the human mind, it is represented by several most important historical phases, and it stands for a distinct, well-defined peculiarity of religious devotion. Mysticism pretends to a more intimate union with God than that which Christian faith ordinarily implies. In the union with God the mystic endeavours to anticipate the fruition of that blessedness which is the state of the redeemed in heaven. It is the catching at something which is beyond the reach of ordinary mortals. The rapture of the mystic is attained only in moments of ecstasy, as the result of special efforts by which he is raised for the time being above himself through intensity of contemplation, fixing the mind upon the divine being, where the feeling of self is lost in the sense of God. The act of mystical union with God implies an abstraction from the world. The world is forgotten, the relation of the man to the world is set aside. If therefore we were to allow that this mystic ecstasy is a legitimate form of devotion, we should have to modify what has been said of the necessary relationship of the Christian to the world. We should have to acknowledge that there is another higher ideal in which the world is left behind, where the religious life consummates itself in the one relation to God. We should be obliged to distinguish between an ordinary, everyday Christianity and the religion of the " perfect." This is, as we well know, what is done. The " religious life " is a higher life than the average Christian life. Christians are divided into two classes: those whose religion is confined within the limits of sober, everyday, Christian experience, and the perfect who alone come to the full fruition of Christian blessedness.

The mystic's religion is abstraction from the

world; Christ's religion is superiority to the world. The two are fundamentally opposed. A religion in which the human is absorbed into the divine and the world is no more, in which a superlative excellence of Christian devotion is sought by means of a transcendental rapture, is foreign to the spirit of the New Testament. It is human, not divine, religion. In the line which it necessarily draws between the ordinary and the perfect it demonstrates its anti-Christian character. The religion of Christ is the world-religion, because it is the religion of all alike. It does indeed count on growth and therefore there are differences of faith. But the same end is accessible to all. There is in the gospels no reservation for the few. There is no esoteric and exoteric. Christianity knows no privileged class. The history of monasticism abundantly proves that there is a peculiar fascination in the "religious" life; but it is the fascination of selfishness, its almost invariable accompaniment is spiritual self-righteousness.

Furthermore, mysticism goes beyond Christ. In that perfect mystical union with God, where the soul is emancipated from time and space, and in an ecstasy of spiritual devotion becomes incorporated in the divine, there is no more Christ, no more positive Christian belief. Christianity becomes a mere stepping-stone to something higher; when that higher is attained, Christianity is done away with. Whereas the true fellowship with God is realised only through Christ. So far as we have any true conception of God it is found only in Christ. Any theory of religion which leaves Christ out steps beyond the bounds of Christianity. Hence it is not surprising to find a close relationship between mysticism and the pagan religions. Mysticism is not Christian, but pagan. It is at home in the theosophies of the East, not in the religion of Christ; its god is the metaphysical god of neo-Platonism, not the God of the New Testament.[1]

Mysticism represents but one of many attempts made at different times in the history of the Christian Church to go beyond the gospel. Monasticism, asceticism, pietism in all its forms, and the Anabaptist extravagances follow the same tendency. They are all alike in this, that they overlay the simplicity of the gospel with elaborations of doctrine or principles.

As efforts to grasp at a higher meaning, to realise a deeper devotion in the Christian religion, such phases of life and belief form an interesting chapter in Church history. They owe their origin to the very greatness of Christianity. The modern view of

[1] A modified type of mysticism traces its origin to the discourses of St. Bernard on the Song of Songs. The Christian's relation to Christ is that of bride and bridegroom. Reverential love of Christ is turned into the play of a morbid phantasy and degraded to a physical passion. To this category belongs to-day the "marriage" of the nun taking the veil to Christ, and the revolting cult of the Sacred Heart. In the same direction lies the morbid contemplation of the sufferings of Christ. "In the Latin Middle Ages the verbal profession of the divinity of Christ is the price paid for the permission to love him as a man, to imitate him as such, to draw him down to one's own level, to play with him" (Ritschl, iii. 553).

life is Christian, it represents the conquest of the world by Christianity. And this view of life has become so thoroughly at home in the world that it is only when we reflect upon it that we recognise its Christian character. Christianity has created the atmosphere of our modern life; but because we have never known any other, we are apt to lose sight of the fact that it is a Christian atmosphere.

It is to this imperfect appreciation of the influence of Christianity in the world that is due the tendency to search for a higher meaning in the Christian religion. The correlate of this tendency is the division which is commonly made between what is called Natural Religion and Revealed Religion. According to this division there are two layers of truth. The lower comprises all that nature, conscience, and the intellect teach; the upper layer is made up of those truths which, being beyond the reach of human faculties, Christ revealed. Among the truths of natural religion is placed the belief in God's providence. This is supposed to be the elementary truth in the Christian religion. It requires no revelation to teach it. We know it of ourselves. The distinctively Christian truths go far beyond it.

It is here more than anywhere else that we discover the inadequacy of our modern religious conceptions. That truth is made the first, the elementary truth, the starting-point, which in reality is the most difficult, which is the last Christian truth, the outcome, the grand conclusion, the ultimate result, the crown of the Christian system.

We speak of the "modern world" as if it were altogether a different world from that of bygone ages. This difference is apt to be exaggerated. And yet there is a truth in the distinction. Our life is different from the life that went before us. What we call "modern civilisation" is modern; the enlightenment, the progress, which we boast of as being a characteristic of these "modern" times, is real. There is a line drawn between the past and the present which is clearly defined. But there is no shallowness so hopelessly shallow as that which attempts to define modern civilisation in terms of material and intellectual achievement. Not a few are dazzled by this kind of success; they identify the progress of our times with the discoveries and inventions and with all those physical accomplishments which have added so much to our knowledge and to the well-being of life.[1] Such do not see that these achievements are merely one manifestation, and that not the most important, of what constitutes the real progress of modern times.

The distinguishing character of modern civilisation is its energy. We find this energy in the intensification of activity along all the lines of human

[1] Compare the display of modern intellectual achievement in Fiske's *Idea of God*. The writer seems to hold that in some unexplained way this intellectual progress has illuminated "the idea of God." Tennyson is wiser in what he says of the "flower in the crannied wall":

". . . if I could understand,
What you are, root and all, and all in all,
I should know what God and man is."

interest. This is true of all that concerns the material welfare of man; it is true also of the intellectual activities. It is furthermore true of certain activities which are equally characteristic of modern "progress," although in their effects they appear rather as a return of the tide of advance. I mean the intensification of political interest and the spread of social agitation among the masses, with the deplorable accompaniment of those evils which books like Bryce's *American Commonwealth* or Lecky's *Liberty and Democracy* bring home to us. Human faculties are keyed to a higher pitch of vigour than ever before: this is modern civilisation.

But is this all? Far from it. He possesses a very meagre knowledge of the true forces which underlie the varying phenomena of human history who fails to discern the motive cause of this increased energy. Underlying all the phenomena of history are great spiritual forces. There has never been a movement but it has been the result of a spiritual force. It is this deeper view of history, which underneath the material effect seeks for the spiritual cause, that is so fascinating to the mind when it has come to a realisation of the fact that all we see on the surface of life is merely the manifestation of the forces underneath. These forces are manifold. Some are easily detected. Such are the love of power, the lust of gold. They are great forces, but there are forces which are greater than these. These are strong in individuals; but to find the motive power in those movements which comprise great masses in their scope, we have to familiarise ourselves with the great spiritual powers.

Underneath the intense energy of the human faculties, underlying the exercise of interest in every line of human progress, is that which alone makes this energy and interest possible, a hopefulness, a buoyancy, a confidence.¹ The more we realise how the mystery of human life, its suffering and death, has hung like a dark cloud over the race, the more we wonder at this confidence and hopefulness. Is it natural ? Here are the words of one of the wisest who lived at the very time Christ came into the world. This is what Pliny the Elder thought of life and its prospects: " The vanity of man, and his insatiable longing after existence, have led him also to dream of a life after death. A being full of contradictions, he is the most wretched of creatures; since the other creatures have no wants transcending the bounds of their nature. Man is full of desires and wants, that reach to infinity, and can never be satisfied. His nature is a lie,—uniting the greatest poverty with the greatest pride. Among these so great evils, the best thing God has bestowed on

¹ It is the energy and the hopefulness of Christianity that struck the intelligent author of the *Diary of a Japanese Convert* most forcibly : " Why is it that heathens in general go into decay so soon, but Christians in general know no decay whatever, but hope even in death itself ? . . . I attribute the progressiveness of Christendom to its Christianity. . . . Enormous yet though their sins are, these people have the power to overcome them. They have yet no sorrows which they think they cannot heal. Is not Christianity worth having if but for this power alone ? " (p. 200.)

man, is the power to take his own life."[1] Here is the true natural theology. With man growing more and more conscious of himself, ever brooding upon the insoluble enigma, his own life, what more natural than that suicide should seem the only true end. Had man given way to the despair of Pliny, it would have been only what might have been expected. Had man in that despair resolved to face his fate bravely, had he steeled himself to bear the inevitable, had he for all these centuries endured to live, that, too, might have been natural, and we should admire the power of resistance implanted in man.[2] But that man, without hope, should develop the intense activity which he displays to-day—this is impossible.

The train of reasoning, whose salient points I have only briefly indicated, must lead to the conclusion that what we call modern civilisation is possible only by virtue of Christianity. Christianity has created the atmosphere of hopefulness which

[1] Pliny's *Natural History*, quoted from Neander's *Church History*, Introduction.
[2] This is the ideal of character represented in Shelley's *Prometheus Unbound*:

" To suffer woes which hope thinks infinite ;
To forgive wrongs darker than death and night ;
To defy power which seems omnipotent ;
To love, and bear : to hope till hope creates
From its own wreck the thing it contemplates ;
Neither to change, nor falter, nor repent ;
This, like thy glory, Titan, is to be
Good, great and joyous, beautiful and free ;
This is alone Life, Joy, Empire, and Victory."

underlies the display of energy that characterises our age. That hopefulness is simply trust in God. Not that this trust exists as an active power in every individual who is energetically active, but it does exist in society at large; it exists as a very positive power in many who consciously believe in a guiding providence. It exists in many more as an unconscious disposition. Take away this trust, and modern civilisation would collapse in a day.[1]

It is because we see this confidence everywhere around us, because we have been brought up in it from our infancy, because we have never known anything else, that we are apt to forget that it owes its being to Christianity, that it would be utterly impossible without Christianity, that in this very

[1] The view here presented is of course diametrically opposed to that which Mr. Spencer maintains with so much force. It is a common infirmity, of two phenomena which are evidently related to one another as cause and effect, to choose that which suits one's own theory for cause and the other for effect, when the relation might just as well be the reverse. In this case it is a very delicate question. Taking religion and practice as two doubtless related phenomena, which is cause and which is effect? Spencer maintains that practice generates religion. "It was not the creed but the mode of life which was influential—not the theory but the practice. This, indeed, is the general reply to be made to the large claim put in for Christianity as the great civilizer, etc." (*Principles of Sociology*, iii. p. 477). The drift of thought has, I think, been away from Mr. Spencer. His mistake is that he does not recognise the religious forces, which exist as unconscious and half-conscious feelings, habits of mind and views of life, and as such are powerful motives of action among the great masses of Christian people. If Christianity were simply the conscious belief in Christian doctrines, it would play a very small part indeed in the world's history.

hopefulness and confidence we find the effect of Christ's work upon earth. And forgetting that, and putting it down to the credit of so-called " Natural Religion," we worry ourselves to find out what Christianity really is and we impose upon ourselves an unnecessary yoke in the shape of an extraordinary exercise of devotion above simple faith.

An objection may be urged to the view, as here stated, that Christianity makes the energy of modern civilisation possible. First, it seems strange, upon this hypothesis, that the faith in God, which we have claimed as eminently the outcome of Christianity, should be nowhere so beautifully expressed as in the Psalter, written long before Christ; so that we to-day still go to the Psalms for the highest embodiment of that faith. Secondly, it is not our age alone that is characterised by an intense energy. What shall we say of the age of Pericles ? Must there not have been a hopefulness and buoyancy to make possible the masterpieces of Greek art—and that without Christianity ?

This is true. The early ages of the world did possess hopefulness and confidence, and among the Hebrews a pronounced and most beautiful faith in God. It is not claimed that either of these could not exist at any period without Christianity. But, had there been no Christianity, there would have come a time when these qualities would have ceased to exist.

Something is due to the freshness of the world in the earlier stages of human history. The life of the human race bears a certain analogy to the life of the individual, in that there is an infancy and a maturity of the race. The characteristic of maturity is self-consciousness. I am aware that it is dangerous rashly to assume a difference of our age from any preceding age. Human nature is alike in all ages; and the phenomena which we hold to be peculiar to our own, a more familiar knowledge of past events often teaches us, have been equally well known in other periods. But we cannot escape this conclusion that the modern world is different from the ancient in its self-consciousness. The mind of man has tended more and more to return upon itself. Not that they did not study the workings of the mind. We remember Plato. But they threw themselves unreservedly into the objective external as we cannot. We are held back by an overpowering sense of personality. It is the difference between heedless childhood and manhood which cannot get away from itself, but is forever pursued by the insistent perplexities of its own mind.

When Christ told his disciples to become like little children, he recognised both the natural bent of the child and the effort which it costs the man to become as the child. The childhood of the human race lacked the sense of independence which belongs to maturity; it found no difficulty in believing a God or many gods, although even then it required, as we believe, a special inspiration to reveal to the Hebrews the truth that God is a God to be trusted. But our self-conscious age, in the sense of its maturity and independence, finds it increasingly difficult to return to the conditions of childhood. It no longer believes as the child believes. The simple child-faith of the Hebrew Psalmist could not have lasted. There would inevitably have stolen over the world the sense of hopeless perplexity and a dark despair such as is portrayed in those words of Pliny, had there not come into our life a something which brings home to man with a coercive force far beyond that of human voice the possibility of that trustfulness of the child, which underlies and alone makes possible our modern civilisation.

The thought which is here dwelt upon is, by a logic which is precisely the reverse of the true, used to make it appear that our time stands less in need of religion than the past ages. Religion, it is said, is a guide for the immature; we have grown into manhood; we dismiss the guide. We have done with it; the world having gone so far with religion, can now do without it. We can see how shallow such talk is, how for the very fact that man has passed out of the stage where he acted spontaneously into the self-conscious stage, in which he probes every motive of his action, he needs religion more than ever to give him the hopefulness which is necessary for life. What would be the result should Christianity disappear from the face of the earth ? Suppose that by some magic there should suddenly come upon men the belief that Christianity is a delusion. The mind is staggered in trying to conceive the catastrophe that would follow the total disappearance of faith. This is certain: what we call civilisation would be no more.

We have been led into the foregoing train of thought by the consideration of what constitutes the essential character of the Christian life. It has been maintained that the faith in God's providence, which gives us security and dominion of the world, is the principle of the eternal life into which we are brought by entering into fellowship with God through the forgiveness of our sins; that this faith in God's providence constitutes the essential character of the Christian life, that therefore nothing beyond it need be sought. And we have tried to show that historically it is this very faith which makes Christianity the supporter of modern civilisation, that this faith is the distinguishing mark of Christianity as a social religion.

In what has been said upon the latter theme it seems to be taken for granted that there exists an unconscious Christianity, a Christianity of those who act from Christian motives, but have not the Christian belief. And so much indeed we must acknowledge. Here, however, it is largely a question of the proper use of terms. I do not know that it would be a very fruitful discussion as to whether those could properly be called Christians who do not consciously believe in Christ. But it is both an interesting and a profitable consideration, that the hopeful outlook upon life which is the only motive of energetic action, which produces growth and improvement in society, is distinctively Christian in its nature.

We can see clearly that there must be a nucleus of conscious believers in Christ. This function belongs to the Christian Church. It is the sphere of those who enter into fellowship with God through Christ. The Christian life in that fellowship is not that poor, negative kind which consumes its energies in trying to avoid sin and falls into the worst of all sins. It is the positive aspiration after an ideal. That ideal is nothing else but the perfect life, the possibility of life which is beckoning every human being, not the narrowness of a so-called " religious " life, essentially selfish, reserved for a few. That ideal is but one for all humanity; we are too weak ever to reach it, but we are strong enough to aspire to it, and it becomes to us a high motive. This is the life which is filled out with the faithful work at life's task as our God-imposed duty, in that state of life unto which it has pleased God to call us; the life which is built upon an unfaltering faith in God's providence; which finds its highest expression in prayer; which approves itself against the world by the practice of patience and humility.

Let us rejoice if God finds his way into the human soul by other means than by Christ. That does not shake our belief that the Church is the divinely appointed means, the sphere in which God has ordained that man should enter into fellowship with him. The Church then is the seat of the power which Christianity has brought into the world; the life of its Christian fellowship is the living influence of Christianity among men. God does not work by magic charms; but he does work by the lives of men. And the life of the true Christian fellowship is the life instinct with the life of Christ; it is the life of fellowship with God based upon forgiveness. In the Church's life is the motive power of Christianity. To it has been committed by God the future of the world. It draws men into itself and by an appeal which is more powerful than any other it opens the way in their hearts for the entrance of God. Is not this the truth of the Saviour's promise: " Whosesoever sins ye forgive they are forgiven them " ? This is the mystery of that strange power above all other powers, the power of human life, so strong in the individual, how much stronger in the Church of Christ. How full of meaning, when we understand this, is not the declaration of absolution at the opening of our Morning Prayer, setting forth as the first act of our worship the forgiveness of sins, to bring which is the proper function of the Church.[1]

The Church is the purveyor of the divine blessing. Its work is not done by magic processes; that is a perversion of Christianity. God's blessing is transmitted through the life of the Church, both the individual life of its members and the life of the whole body. There is a real life of the Church dis-

---

[1] It was perhaps the worst fault of Puritanism that it lost sight of the true function of the Church. The body, ordained by Christ for the execution of his mission, became a voluntary association of like-minded people.

tinct from the life of its members. It makes itself especially felt in the worship of the Church. The worship of the Church is the act of the whole body, not of the individual.

There are two ideas of worship. According to one I go to Church for what I can get out of Church; in every act of the public function I stand as an individual before God; I pray for myself, I praise for myself; I listen to the Bible and to the preaching for myself. This is the very negation of the Church's function and the ignoring of the true idea of Christian worship. This idea is nothing if not the expression of fellowship. The worship is *common* worship; it is pervaded above all with the feeling of sympathy and one common aim; its essential character is not petition or instruction, but praise. Man's true worship of God is the praise of God.

The common worship is the highest act of the Christian life. It is that act which is most instinct with vitality and energy. We have all felt the great power there is in common worship, when that worship is genuine. There is no spiritual force comparable to that of true united worship, voices raised in harmony of tone and harmony of spirit in the praise of God. It throws out an irresistible spell. It is the most powerful means at the disposal of the Church for the spread of the kingdom of God. There is a convincing force in common worship, bringing home the truths of God's fatherhood and man's brotherhood, which no logic can hope to equal. Selfishness cannot stand against it.

When the Church is engaged in the act of true worship, she is the Church of Christ indeed.

But, alas! is this true worship the worship of the Church which has inscribed upon her book of worship " Common Prayer" ? Or must she acknowledge that she has not been faithful to her highest function? Is it not time that we should set ourselves in all seriousness to answer this question: *What is Christian worship?* Are we hopelessly blind to the fact that the act of praise performed by a set of appointed functionaries is in no sense of the word the worship of the congregation? The performance of the concert hall never can be the praise of the Church. Before Almighty God there is no such thing as vicarious worship. An abuse, which has not its equal in the life of the Church, which will more and more destroy the vital influence of the Church in America, has been allowed to take root and grow. Our congregations have almost ceased to worship, and rest in the comfortable belief that they do their duty to God if they have delegated that most essential function of the Christian to a set of appointed singers. Even that most solemn act of Christian worship, the profession of our common faith, is turned into a show-performance, at which the congregation takes the part of an audience at the opera—a very satire upon our " common prayer."[1]

[1] There is no part of our Church life to-day which so cries out for reform as the public worship. On the title-page of our prayer-book stand the words, " Common Prayer." At the opening of our morn-

We have spent much of our time and energy in trying to find out what was the original constitution of the Church. Would it not be well if we now turned our thoughts to the great living reality, the Church in our own time, and endeavoured to understand what is its God-ordained use, what is the power entrusted to it, how does that power manifest itself, and what stands in the way of its operation? It is an inspiring thought that this organisation is the instrument chosen of God for the redemption of mankind, and there is a glorious field for the Church's work. But that work will be adequately done only when the selfishness of sectarian individ-

ing service is this appeal: "O come, let us sing unto the Lord: let us heartily rejoice in the strength of our salvation. . . . O come, let us worship and fall down. . . . O worship the Lord in the beauty of holiness." What, measured by the standard of these expressions, shall we say of the worship as it is generally performed in our churches? Either a set of hired singers performs an elaborate musical programme for the entertainment of a very few musical people, and the church is degraded to the level of a music hall; or the congregation stands listlessly waiting for the end of a dreary chant in which it takes not the slightest part. Let who will deceive himself with the absurdity of a "worship of the heart"; true worship has well-nigh gone out of the Church, to the infinite loss of her vital power. For—and I challenge anyone to deny this—the recital of music by a choir is not Christian worship. The word "Common Prayer" is becoming a misnomer. A more appropriate title for our service book would be, "The Book of Prayers, together with a libretto of the customary musical recitals." The apathy of the Church in this matter, the almost entire neglect of the latent powers of worship in our Book of Common Prayer, is in these days of humanitarian enthusiasm a most extraordinary phenomenon. When will the time come that we shall learn the difference between a church and a concert hall?

ualism, such as turns common worship into a parody, gives way to a larger feeling of a common life and common aspirations.

At no period has the Church failed in the performance, in some degree, of her divinely appointed task, or else society would long ago have crumbled. Yet it seems, as we look around us to-day, as if the Christian Church had not yet awakened to the full consciousness that her supreme mission, as the Church militant, is to build up virile, brave, hopeful character, and so doing to lay the foundations for that society which shall ever advance towards the consummation of the kingdom of God upon earth. Let the Church to-day reflect that the splendid practical work which she is doing will prove unsubstantial in proportion as she fails of the appointed function of the Church: to show to the world what it is to be forgiven, to live near God, to hold up to the world the ideal of the eternal life. If to-day we have to acknowledge a deflection from that ideal, I believe the chief cause is in the degeneracy of our worship.

In concluding this part of our enquiry, let us turn to the writings of those who are the true Christian prophets and seers of our day, the great modern poets: a Tennyson, a Browning, a Wordsworth. What is the secret of that power which makes us so often sit at their feet ? Is it not that they have preached a message which, bringing in a larger hope and a stronger faith, sustains us and gives us courage? And that message, whence did they get it? Can there be a doubt?

When at the close of the first book of the "*Excursion*" we read how the wanderer's meditations at the deserted cottage taught him,

> " That what we feel of sorrow and despair
> From ruin and from change, and all the grief
> That passing shows of Being leave behind,
> Appeared an idle dream, that could maintain
> Nowhere, dominion o'er the enlightened spirit
> Whose meditative sympathies repose
> Upon the breast of Faith,"

we read in language as beautiful as any that English literature contains the expression of a faith which was drawn from Christ.

But Browning, too. Those inspiring lines:

> " Therefore to whom turn I but to Thee, the ineffable Name,
> Builder and maker, Thou, of houses not made with hands!
> What, have fear of change from Thee who art ever the same?
> Doubt that Thy power can fill the heart that Thy power expands?
> There shall never be one lost good! What was, shall live as before ;
> The evil is null, is nought, is silence implying sound ;
> What was good, shall be good, with, for evil, so much good more :
> On the earth the broken arks ; in the heaven, a perfect round."

—they carry the message of faith, of courage, of hopefulness. Could those words ever have been penned without Christianity? They go right to the heart of the Christian religion. Whatever Browning's intellectual belief was, he learned that lesson from Christ.

" Doubt that Thy power can fill the heart that

Thy power expands?" Contrast that with Pliny: "His nature is a lie,—uniting the greatest poverty with the greatest pride."

Take even the poetry of an agnostic like Matthew Arnold. With a music of its own, it often breathes the spirit of the genuine seer. However little conscious he was of it, that spirit came to him from no other source than Christianity. Could "Rugby Chapel" or "Self-Dependence" ever have been written in an atmosphere of pure agnosticism?[1]

We do not like to acknowledge it, but we turn for comfort and strength far more to the poets than we do to more professedly Christian writings. But our instincts are true, because we recognise in their message more than in many a volume of sermons the ring of genuine Christian faith. And the reason of this is that the poet, with that intuition which is his gift, goes straight to the heart of Christianity, and the simplicity of his message comes to us with an irresistible appeal. The theologian often for the

---

[1] How great is the debt which American Christianity owes to our American poets: a Bryant, a Whittier, a Longfellow, a Lowell. But where are the hands that shall grasp the torch from these giants and pass the light of truth and hope to the coming generations? I was on the point of adding Emerson's name to the list. But, with all his exquisite refinement of thought, is not the strong note of the prophet quite wanting in him? No wonder that his appreciation of Christianity was small. Compare his lines in "Song of Nature":

> "One in a Judean manger,
> And one by Avon stream,
> One over against the mouths of Nile,
> And one in the Academe."

very trees sees not the forest; he labours to set before us a Christianity which is too often artificial, which fails to satisfy the deep yearning of the heart for the heavenly food.

But we are learning a truer theology. The old forms of interpretation, which in their day were the embodiment of new and valuable truth, are giving way before a larger knowledge. A deeper insight and a keener sympathy for the needs of man is opening before our eyes larger vistas of truth.

In this Christian receptiveness we recognise the vitality of the Christian religion. The truth " once delivered to the saints " remains ever the same, an absolute constant ideal. But the Christian's theology, his understanding and appreciation of that truth, is ever growing and we trust will never cease to grow.

CHAPTER IV.

THE IDEA OF GOD.

ALL theological systems consistently carried out centre in the idea of God. Underlying every religious problem we find in the last analysis this question: How do we conceive of God? The theological enquirer, when he begins his investigation, necessarily starts with some conception of God. This will be at first more or less dim and undetermined. It is the result of various forces that have acted upon him: training, observation of life, the Bible. As he proceeds to define and harmonise the various elements, the idea of God becomes more and more clarified, until finally the system comes to rest in a representation of God that will satisfy all the elements of the problem in his own mind. You know that the water in the stream comes from high up in the hills. Far down its course you judge from the colour and the taste somewhat of the nature of the soil from which it springs. But you are not satisfied until you have traced it back to its source and stand at last where it gushes out of the ground. So, all the while we were studying the working of those spiritual powers under whose influence we stand, we were conscious that they proceeded from a source high above us. Now we must trace the stream to that source and press as near as possible into the presence of the Fountain-head of all power.

It is the fault of a great deal of our theology that it starts with those conceptions of God which are supposed to be natural to man. It therefore takes as the foundation of its idea, not the conceptions of an enlightened Christian sense, but those general notions common to all humanity. It seeks its knowledge of the Deity as far as possible from Christianity, among the sages of ancient Greece or in the intuitive notions of uncivilised tribes. Hence those terms which are so much heard: the " infinite being," the " absolute," the " great first cause." The full conception of God is therefore made up of two strata, the one pagan, the other Christian. The one is a conglomerate of metaphysical conceptions, the other is an appendix of Christian ideas.

This incongruous mixture of conceptions is due to the hold which Greek philosophy had upon the great minds of the Church almost from the beginning. The early Greek theology was saturated with metaphysical elements which prevented the Christian revelation from maintaining the constitutive importance that properly belongs to it in a consistent Christian system. We learn to know God truly only through the Christian revelation. Instead of starting with a general idea of God and rising from that to the particular Christian conception, we begin and end with the Christian God, we know no other God than the God of Christ.

It is at this point particularly that we apply the principle which differentiates religious from theoretical knowledge, as it was set forth in the introductory chapter. The organ of religious knowledge is not the pure intellect. We judge religious questions not by a pure mental judgment, but by the value of those feelings that accompany the mental act. We cannot know God as he is in himself, but we can know him for what he is to *us*, by the value which he has for us. There is no such thing as a disinterested knowledge of God. This was the fatal misconception which the early theologians inherited from the Greek philosophy. My ideas of God are rightly governed by the interests of my spiritual life, by the need which I have of a God.

What is that need ? What purpose is the conception of God intended to serve ? There must be a practical reason why we believe in God, why we cannot be without God. That reason will be the touchstone of all our ideas about God, will govern and regulate all our thought of God.

To the philosopher and the scientist it may be a curious question, what he is to think of the origin of this material world. If theology is prompted by mere curiosity, it is not conscious of its true function. Its interest is wholly different. It starts from man's nature and finds that it is incomplete without God. The conditions of life demand a God. It is a practical matter to the theologian. Man needs God not to explain life—for the explanation of life is a secondary interest to him—but to make life possible.

Man needs God to make life possible for two reasons. First is the ethical reason. The terms expressive of moral value, duty, responsibility, justice, etc., have no meaning unless there is something behind them. The idea of God must be such that it renders these terms intelligible, it must give value to ethical quantities. This is the first test of our idea of God. The second test is distinctively religious. It concerns man's natural condition of dependence. Man finds himself placed in a position of apparently hopeless contradiction. He is a part of nature, subject like all other material things, to the unchangeable laws of the universe. Looking at himself from this point of view, he seems a mere plaything in the hands of overwhelming forces, utterly helpless. On the other hand, he cannot escape the consciousness of a something within him which raises him above the world. He has an inborn sense of the dignity of his human nature, a conviction that his life represents a superior value. There is within him a feeling of superiority, the stamp of a preference which marks him as heir to a destiny transcending nature. This contradiction in the life of man is insoluble without God. We need God to read the riddle of our life, to secure our place in the world.

This is the twofold test which is to be the criterion of all our thoughts about God. The God we are to believe in must assure us that in the distinction we make between right and wrong, as well as in the value which we put upon our own life, we shall not in the end be brought to confusion. Whatever conception we form of God, it must perform for us this double service. The question now is: Whence shall we derive the knowledge of God which will satisfy these two conditions?

It was stated above that the great fault of the traditional theology was that it derived its fundamental conceptions of God from reason, or so-called natural theology. The force of this criticism will be seen, if we apply to the God of natural theology the tests which have been set forth. We shall therefore proceed to the examination of the various arguments for the existence of God.

First are the three metaphysical arguments: the cosmological, teleological, and ontological. The cosmological argument reasons from the conditioned to the unconditioned. All that we know in the material word is conditioned. The conditioned postulates a series of conditions until the unconditioned is reached. Therefore behind the conditioned universe we must assume an unconditioned being—God. The teleological argument reasons from design to a designer. All parts of the world give evidence of design. We are forced to assume an almighty Designer—God. This argument is supposed to have lost its force by the discovery of the principle of evolution. In fact, however, it needs only to be remodelled and it retains whatever force belonged to it. The ontological argument deals with pure concepts of the mind. The conception of the highest possible being which the mind is capable of forming carries with it the existence of that being. If he did not exist he would be wanting in perfection. Therefore God exists.

These are the time-honoured arguments for the existence of a supreme being. What sort of a God do they set up? Here is the point where grave mistakes are made. Conclusions are anticipated to which we have no right. A bare philosophical abstraction is surreptitiously clothed with the attributes of the being whom we call God. Whereas all we have gained is a vague notion of an "unconditioned," an "absolute," a "self-existent being," an "original intelligence"—an utterly barren idea.

The metaphysical arguments are indeed nothing more than an analysis of that concept of the mind in which we represent God to ourselves. It is the consciousness of a something behind phenomena. All therefore that these terms do for us is to suggest that there is somewhere an adequate solution for this riddle of a world, the source of whose being and the manner of whose existence are absolutely beyond the reach of our mental powers. But that we know without the subtlety of metaphysical reasoning.

Kant gave to the metaphysical conception of God a more practical meaning. Our mental processes postulate the idea of God as the "ideal of the pure reason." The metaphysical God is the logical condition of all reasoning, the necessary assumption of all thought. Our reason demands a God. That does not prove the existence of God. But man is obliged by the necessity of his mental faculties to conceive of a something behind reason which gives reality to reason; he must reason as if there were a God.

Let us now apply to the metaphysical conception of God the tests which we have adopted as necessary for our judgment upon any conception of God, its ethical and spiritual value. Measured by this twofold test, the metaphysical conception of God, either in the traditional or the Kantian form, is worthless. The metaphysical and the religious idea of God are widely different. The metaphysical God has no ethical value; it affords no ground for moral distinctions. Neither has it spiritual contents. The very suggestion of a religious trust in such a logical abstraction is preposterous. The metaphysical God is not the sort of God we want. It is useless to us. It is a God in whom the devils believe, although they do not even tremble at him—a colourless abstraction of the mind.

When we pass from the metaphysical to the moral argument, we are carried a step further. This argument starts from the existence of moral sentiments; they make it necessary to assume a fountain-head of morality—God.

We are familiar with that view which makes the moral law equally with everything else the result of evolution. Doubtless we owe to the distinguished scientists who have treated this theme, especially Mr. Herbert Spencer, a great clarification of our ideas about the contents of many of our moral conceptions. We must allow that in their substance many, if not all of these, are the results of experience. This is true of parental responsibility for children, the rights of property, the sanctity of life. These sentiments have grown up as a result of the exigencies of society, through a course of evolution which has been proceeding for untold ages under the impulse of the struggle for existence. And we have not yet reached the goal of moral evolution. As we go forward and adapt ourselves more completely to the conditions of progress, we evolve new moral sentiments. Christianity has produced many such, and I shall have occasion later on to point out the direction in which we may expect higher conceptions of ethical obligation to be evolved in the future.

But that does not touch the core of the moral question. Evolution cannot explain the cogency of the moral imperative. I can understand how the obligation to speak the truth developed as the result of a long experience, proving that truth was necessary for the existence of society. But your argument does not prove to me why the voice of conscience commands me individually, me personally, me specifically, to speak nothing but the truth.

It is not infrequently assumed, with an extraordinary superficiality of observation, that the traditional supernatural sanctions for moral conduct, while well enough in their day, are no longer needed. They have served their purpose, and, like the scaffolding which held the stones of the arch while it was building, now that it is finished, may be thrown away.

The very reverse is true. The sanctions of an ethical system are more needed to-day than ever. I have said, in a preceding chapter, that we of our day differ in nothing so much from the men of past centuries as in our greater self-consciousness. In the earlier ages men used to act without thinking. They did not care much about laws and sanctions. Habit governed. Once started, they moved unthinkingly along the same track. It did not make much difference to them whether there was any reason for acting in one particular way rather than in another. They were used to it; that was all. Not so now. We stop and look back and ask, Are we on the right track? We want to have a reason for everything that we do, and if no adequate reason can be given we will stop doing that particular thing. So, among other things, a reason is demanded for the cogency of the moral law. It has been attempted to give such. We may safely say that at this point the historical method completely breaks down. A little reflection must convince the candid student how utterly inadequate experience is to furnish sanctions for right conduct. If I see a gold piece belonging to another man and am absolutely certain that I can take it without being detected, no amount of argumentation upon the naturalistic hypothesis will avail to convince me that I *ought* not to take it. What do I care for the good of *society?* What are *coming generations* to me? I want my own good. Doing right is something more than a habit, and there is a reason other than the good of " society " or of "humanity." Underlying the vast complexus of human institutions, habits, and motives, which we call modern civilisation, there is the sense of the eternal validity of truth, apart from and beyond all experience. If this did not exist, civilisation would collapse in a day.[1]

In the *Data of Ethics* there is a curious passage which shows that the author himself felt the need of a higher sanction than that which mere experience gives to good conduct. We read, at the end of Chapter IX.: "The intuitions corresponding to these (moral) sentiments, have, in virtue of their origin, a general authority to be *reverently* recognised." In the use of language the object of reverence is conceived as above us. Mr. Spencer cannot quite get away from the idea that moral sanctions must, after all, come from a sphere above experience.

There is indeed something exquisitely self-contradictory in constructing a system of ethics, while claiming that it is all "evolved." How much deeper are the investigations into the springs of morality made by Immanuel Kant! He saw the

---

[1] I think there is a pretty general agreement that we have gone beyond the position of Mr. Spencer. One cannot take up one of the treatises written by men of his school, without being strongly impressed by two things: first, what a wonderful clue to the understanding of the world this theory of evolution is; secondly, how utterly it breaks down when it is used as a key to the understanding of man's spiritual and moral nature, to solve the highest problems of humanity. There is an x whose mystery the keenest historical analysis fails to touch.

impossibility of a morality without God. Says Kant: " Such a ruler (God), together with life in such a world, which we must consider as future, reason compels us to admit, unless all moral laws are to be considered as idle dreams, because, without that supposition, the necessary consequences, which the same reason connects with these laws, would be absent." (*Pure Reason*, Müller's translation, p. 696). Kant's argument is based upon the assumption that ethical action is possible only through the belief in the ultimate coincidence of happiness and goodness. And this is impossible without God. The ethical law in man makes it necessary to postulate God. This does not establish the *existence* of God. Only we must *think* God. Kant makes the well-known distinction between practical and theoretical necessity. Practically, you act as if there were a God. Theoretically, you have no right to say there is a God.

In the preface to his *Types of Ethical Theory*, Mr. James Martineau illustrates by his own experience the cogency of the ethical sentiments. He is speaking of the motives which induced him to abandon the determinist position: " It was the irresistible pleading of the moral consciousness which first drove me to rebel against the limits of the merely scientific conception. . . . The secret misgivings which I had always felt at either discarding or perverting the terms which constitute the vocabulary of character,—' responsibility,' ' guilt,' ' merit,' ' duty,'— came to a head, and insisted upon speaking out and being heard; and to their reiterated question, 'Is there then no *ought to be* other than *what is?*' I found the negative answer of Diderot intolerable, and all other answers impossible." The force of the moral argument is here most admirably expressed. "The irresistible pleading of the moral consciousness" is the stumbling-block to all naturalistic theories of morality.

Kant maintained that God must be postulated to make thought possible; but that does not establish the existence of God. The same condition holds for conduct. But here we must go a step further. It makes no difference to the mental processes whether there really is a God or not. The man who believes in God and the man who does not, follow the same rules of thought. Not so in action. It will ultimately make a very great difference in conduct whether man believes in God or not. The practical issues of life force us to a decision. We are driven by the imperative demands of our situation to enquire why right is right and wrong is wrong. "The irresistible pleading of the moral consciousness" brings home the question which must be answered: Can we believe in an eternal God, the author and source of moral distinctions?

I ask myself, what is goodness, justice, truth? Are they mere convenient means to an end, and that end not myself, but society, mankind? If so, then I cannot see why that man should not be accounted wisest who makes cunning the ruling principle of his life, the cunning which circumvents the arbitrary laws by which future generations are made the chief beneficiaries of good actions, and grasps all it can for itself. The moral sense revolts from such a conclusion.

We question whether Kant might not have gone farther than he did. We are tempted to say that the moral nature of man not only demands a God, but proves a God. Kant, however, is right. We have no complete proof. If we argued from the moral sense to God and then accepted him because he satisfies the moral sense, we should be reasoning in a circle. We shall see that the Kantian argument leaves the completion of the proof to religion.

In themselves, both the metaphysical and the moral argument are incomplete. But they are not valueless. They reveal to us the need man has of a God. The intellectual nature is incomprehensible without God. The moral faculty is a delusion if there is no God. And to these we can add a third. The spiritual nature of man craves a God. The Psalmist's cry: " My soul is athirst for God, yea, even for the living God " voices the universal longing. It is the cry that goes up, wherever there is a human heart quick with the sense of human wants,

> " From the spirits on earth that adore,
> From the souls that entreat and implore,
>   In the fervour and passion of prayer ;
> From the hearts that are broken with losses
> And weary with dragging the crosses
>   Too heavy for mortals to bear."

Look at humanity from the side of its accomplishments, taking human nature as we see it on the surface of life, and nothing is easier than to slide into the cynic's vein: man is so ignoble, so deceitful, so selfish. But penetrate beneath the surface, learn to know man on the side of his aspirations, and you see him tending up, groping, reaching out, grasping at the higher, striving to know God,

> " Like plants in mines which never saw the sun,
> But dream of him, and guess where he may be,
> And do their best to climb and get to him."

We shall now have to take up another train of thought, which has not perhaps received the consideration it may claim. Natural theology is bound to take account of a certain class of evidence in nature, which seems to point in a direction different from that in which we look for a solution of our problem. I mean the evidence of history and biology. It properly belongs to the teleological argument. We conclude from universal adaptation to an intelligent author. What shall we conclude of God from the suffering in the world? When the individual suffers or sees others, apparently innocent, suffer, his faith in the goodness of God receives a shock. What shall we say when a great catastrophe sweeps away hundreds and thousands of the innocent as well as the guilty? Modern investigation has vastly extended our knowledge of the laws of life; and when we come to understand that the universal law of life is the survival of the fittest, and that in obedience to this law there is a never-ceasing battle for life, that in this battle innocence and good intentions are of no account; when we see how the great machinery of life is arranged with a single eye to the welfare and the advance of the race and there is not the least care of the individual; when, in the light of these cruel laws, we contemplate the awful spectacle of human suffering and the terrible prodigality and carelessness of life—the conclusion seems forced upon us that the author of all this must be a being devoid of moral quality and indifferent to human welfare, that he can have no love for the individual. It cannot be denied that these reflections tell heavily. The God of nature is not the God who rewards the good and punishes evildoers, or one whom we can trust, upon whom we can depend to uphold us against the world.

"Natural Theology" is bound to take not only a part but the whole of the teachings of nature, and nature includes history and biology. The facts which these studies furnish may well startle those who have looked to natural theology as the underpinning of Christianity. If nature is supposed to have revealed God, we can hardly help recoiling from the spirit we have raised. We need another God who will save us from the God of nature.[1]

[1] The idea of the education of the human race, to which appeal has been so frequently made, is helpless to save us from the dilemma in which the apparently remorseless cruelty of nature's God places us. We are asked to derive comfort from the reflection that the tendency of things is towards a millennial perfection of human nature and society. Mankind is conceived as a sort of pyramid, the pinnacle of

There is one exception to this forbidding teaching of nature; one word which she speaks gives us a hope of something better. It is only a delicate suggestion, but to those who are sensitive to the subtle intimations which God gives of himself, it is sufficient. This is the existence of beauty.

In studying the history of man upon earth, we find that one law reigns supreme: the law of adaptation. Everything has its use, every faculty in man serves its purpose in adding to his advantages in the inexorable struggle for existence. At first it was a question of physical powers; the battle was to the swift and the strong. Then there came a time when intellectual pre-eminence began to tell, and the powers of the mind have since been decisive factors in the absorbing struggle. Every faculty was given man for the one purpose. Even the highest of them, the power of sympathy, takes its place in the series of means with which man is furnished for the purpose of raising himself. It represents the law which steps in to take the place of the lower law of the mere struggle for existence, when man has reached an advanced stage of civilisation. Only

---

which represents the perfected society. But there is poor comfort in the idea of a God who can condemn incalculable multitudes of human beings to suffering and death just that they may be the stepping-stones to the perfected happiness of a comparatively insignificant number. True, history points unmistakably to the pyramidal idea of human society. Religion rests upon the infinite value of each individual composing the lower as well as the higher strata of the pyramid. Here is the ultimate antithesis of the psychological and the historical views. Will the mind of man ever solve it?

the sense of beauty has no function to perform in the struggle for existence. It is an end in itself. Upon the utilitarian theory we ask in vain for an answer to the question: What is the purpose of the appreciation of beauty which is implanted in man?[1]

Here, then, is something in ourselves which points beyond this world, which has the mark of eternity. We receive at last an intimation of what man was made for. For this love of beauty in us is not left unsatisfied. See how nature treats man here. She has left his moral needs unfulfilled. Not so his craving for the beautiful. She has moulded things in heaven and things on earth in forms of beauty, and has touched the sky and the sea and the land with colours, in which his highest faculty finds satisfaction. In that satisfaction we recognise the promise from God of immortality and another world. It is something more than poetic rapture, it is the expression of a deep truth, when Hawthorne exclaims:[2]

---

[1] I believe the sense of beauty is supposed to have served as a factor in "natural selection." But this does not impair the truth of what is said in the text. For while that use diminishes with advancing civilisation, the sense of beauty increases.

The train of thought in the text serves to show the folly of the exclusively altruistic view of life. It is often taken for granted that activity for others is the highest possible exercise of the human faculties; and one not infrequently hears expressions as if this was the only life worth living. Whoever lives in that spirit is making but a poor preparation for heaven, where surely there will be no more work for others and where, if we have not done so here, we shall have to learn to employ our faculties in a manner which will bring its own immediate satisfaction.

[2] *Mosses From an Old Manse*, "The Old Manse."

"Our Creator would never have made such lovely days and have given us the deep hearts to enjoy them, above and beyond all thought, unless we were meant to be immortal. This sunshine is the golden pledge thereof. It gleams through the gates of paradise and shows us glimpses far inward." It is the lesson which Wordsworth learned from nature, as he tells us in his description of the Wanderer:

> "——he had felt the power
> Of Nature, and already was prepared
> By his intense conceptions, to receive
> Deeply the lesson deep of love which he
> Whom Nature, by whatever means, has taught
> To feel intensely, cannot but receive."

The existence of beauty in nature is a hint, an intimation, of something beyond. Nature furnishes no proof of God, and natural theology would be a delusion but for the fact that it makes clear the sort of God man needs. Its claim to furnish the foundation for the conception of what God is, of being a factor in the Christian conception of God, is an unwarranted assumption. On the contrary, if we are to find the God we want, it must be one with attributes the very opposite of those to which nature chiefly gives evidence.

We turn therefore to the only other source of possible knowledge: Revelation. From natural religion we advance to revealed religion. We shall first try to answer the question, What is the Christian idea of God? And we shall then measure this idea by the two tests which we have adopted.

The popular Christian conception of God is dualistic. Two attributes claim equal consideration. On the one side is God's justice or righteousness. It is that quality which is generally identified with the first person of the Trinity. This attribute is fundamental. It expresses what is central in the being of God. Whatever we conceive of God's dealings with his creatures must be corrected by the criterion of his primary attribute of justice. On the other side is God's love. This is generally associated with Christ. It is an effort of which the theological mind has not usually been capable, to carry back this attribute of love into the being of the Father. The dualism shows its weakness here at the start. Whatever may be held in strict theory—we shall presently come to that—in practice, that is, in the theology of everyday use and in the minds of most men, justice is associated with the Father, love with the Son.

The biblical authority for the conception of God, which makes justice his fundamental attribute, is drawn mainly from the Old Testament. Ritschl has attempted to show that the word "righteousness," so much used of God in the Old Testament, denotes that characteristic according to which God acts in strict conformity to his purpose of upholding his covenant with Israel against all enemies, and is therefore synonymous with love.[1] Although his exegesis is frequently forced, and therefore is not convincing, yet he has adduced sufficient proof to oblige us to modify our ideas of the use of this term.

[1] Vol. ii. chap. 14.

It is frequently used where justice would not be an exact equivalent, but where it conveys nearly the same conception as love or mercy. So in Psalm xxxi. 1: "In thee, O Lord, have I put my trust; let me never be put to confusion: deliver me in thy *righteousness*," and Psalm xxxvi. 10: "O continue forth thy loving-kindness unto them that know thee, and thy *righteousness* unto them that are true of heart." Exegesis is not, however, the decisive factor in the determination of the Christian idea of God, and the Old Testament is not the Christian's primary authority. We shall presently see that a more exact definition of revelation is required for the solution of the problem of God.

The idea of God and that which depends upon it, the ethical order of the universe, as it is expressed in the commonly accepted view, is founded upon the analogy of the state. God represents the authority of the state. We as his creatures are bound to recognise and observe his laws; this is the condition of eternal life. Representing the supreme power of the state, God is bound not only to reward man for his obedience, but also to punish him for his disobedience. This is the double retribution, by reward and punishment. I have already pointed out the danger of the use of analogy in matters of religion. The likeness which has been thoughtlessly accepted, between God and a human judge or lawgiver, has so fixed the conception of God that it is exceedingly difficult to prove that this conception, resting upon an imperfect analogy, is inadequate.

It is this analogy which gives to the conception the appearance of necessity. We have been so accustomed to thinking of God under the forms of a human state, as the supreme power in a human commonwealth, that we have come to regard any other way of conceiving him as impossible. The analogy has melted into the thing itself. But there is another analogy which Christ used far more frequently, that of fatherhood; and if we can accustom ourselves to follow his thoughts, abandoning Old Testament and Greek precedents, we shall gain quite a different conception of God.

God's justice stands for a certain limitation of his power. He could not do that which love would prompt him to do; there is a bar to his own action. This seems on the face of it to impose a restriction upon God which is inconsistent with his omnipotence. To obviate this objection, it is said that the justice which prevents God's free forgiveness is a part of the nature of God himself; that the bar to his free action springing from his own essential nature is not an inconsistency in our conception of God. God's justice is therefore thought of as analogous to what in man we term honour or self-respect, that quality which carries with it the sense of man's own worth, the strength and persistence of his personality. This fundamental quality, constituting the essential personality of God, must be satisfied; God's love cannot act in disregard of it.

The first objection to this is that justice, as so

conceived, is inapplicable to God. The qualities of personal honour and self-respect are unthinkable except as involving a certain relationship to other beings. And the fundamental condition of this relationship is equality. Honour and self-respect obtain only among equals. Therefore it is impossible to apply them to the being who is supreme above man.

Again, it is impossible to deduce the redemption from God as an act of justice except by inadmissible assumptions. Such is that not uncommon application of physical analogy. A certain rough, popular theology treats God's love and justice as if they were physical objects, two parts of God's nature, lying side by side, between which it is easy to arrange a barter. But when we conceive God's nature by the only applicable analogy, that of human nature, we are forced to acknowledge the impossibility of a theory which, when we cancel theological tergiversation, simply amounts to this, that God placated himself. God desired to save man from sin and death: that desire proceeded from his love. But his justice prevents him; it demands to be satisfied before the intention of love can be carried out. There is no being outside of God who can satisfy it. Therefore God's love, by sending Christ into the world, satisfies God's justice. This can be stated in words, as any other proposition; it can be believed, as any other statement can be believed. But made intelligible to the human mind, we must frankly acknowledge it cannot be.

In Professor Fisher's recent work on the *History of Christian Doctrine* there is an interesting description of an attempt by the late Horace Bushnell to make this theory of the atonement intelligible. He constructs a theory of propitiation by psychological analysis:[1] "It had struck him that in all cases of heavy grievance, even though there is a placable wish and intent, it is psychologically impossible to quiet the resentful retributive impulse inherent in one's own conscience, save by undertaking some work involving loss and suffering in behalf of the offender. Only by this means is the feeling of forgiveness realized in the heart of the party wronged . . . Accordingly God himself in Christ enters upon a work of self-sacrifice and self-propitiation . . . he appeases his own justly indignant sentiment." This is certainly a very acute analysis. Its validity, however, hangs upon one point, about which there is serious question. The "resentful, retributive impulse" which must be "propitiated" is assumed to be "inherent in one's own conscience." But when we reflect how common it is to assign a very mistaken value to one's own feelings, we are led to question whether this "resentful, retributive impulse" is not rather the expression of a human sinful weakness. Should that be the case, then if the man is able to overcome his natural resentful inclination by "undertaking some work involving loss and suffering in behalf of the offen-

[1] This theory is known to me only through Professor Fisher's book.

der," it is evidence that he has gained the victory in a struggle between his better and his worse self. But upon this supposition to argue a "resentful, retributive impulse" in God would be to attribute to him human weakness. We are confirmed in our belief that this is the more correct interpretation of the human feelings by applying our test of God. Can we put our trust in a God whom we believe to be actuated by a "resentful, retributive impulse"? The heart and the mind find no rest in such a God. No such psychological analysis can cover up the fatal dualism of this conception of God.

From the impossibility of conceiving God's justice and his love as existing side by side we are obliged to take refuge in one of the two following positions: Either justice, being the fundamental quality, is a power above God, to which he is subject; it would then be conceived as the mysterious Fate of Greek mythology, exercising a controlling influence over the Deity. Or else, God being thought of as the impersonation of justice, who for his own righteousness' sake cannot waive any of the rigidity of his law, the redemption must be understood as a change effected in God's action through a motive from without. This is done by Christ's "merit." Christ's service for man makes it possible for God to pardon human sin. Christ, as it were, wins pardon from God. But, as man could not possibly by his own merit effect this end, Christ must be more than man, he is divine. The result is,—two Gods.

The first alternative, therefore, is a God above the

God of revelation, the other is two equal Gods. There seems to be no escape. It is worse than useless to delude ourselves in order to maintain a theory which has the stamp of orthodoxy and the prestige of a high pedigree. The argumentation which is resorted to to make this theory seem rational offers mere plausibility for convincing proof. We are concerned here with the most sacred interests of religion. We stand upon the holiest of grounds. Here to resort to self-deception argues surely a shallowness of feeling which is as unworthy of man as it is irreverent to God. Let us remember that we are seeking a theoretical basis for our practical needs. We are reasoning backwards from the wants which we feel to what we must understand as necessary if those wants are to be satisfied. When a man, in the stress of life's experience, throws his trust upon the power to which he looks up as God, he does not stop to enquire into the nature of that power. But such is the craving of our intellectual nature, that in moments of reflection we are impelled to bring our theory into harmony with our practice. And we do not feel that we completely satisfy our own wants until we have learned to think such a God as our minds, as well as our hearts, can rest upon in confidence and trust. It is perfectly possible, upon the traditional or any other assumptions, to construct an idea of God which shall be logical and entirely harmonious in all its parts; but if it is simply the idea of *a* God and not *my* God, it is of no value. I want to know how I am to think of *my* God, the God who speaks to me,

with whom I enter into fellowship, who forgives my
sins, who is my strength and support. This is the
meaning of the tests we have recognised. They are
the practical criteria of thought; they are to prevent
it from losing itself in profitless abstractions, looking
for a foreign God; they are to keep it directed upon
the only God that has any interest for me, and that
is *my* God.

The mind in its search for such a God comes to
rest only in a definition which does violence to no
human feeling. This cannot be said of that God
whom we have to conceive of under two contradictory attributes. It has been shown that such dualism leads us to one of three positions: either a God
that is unthinkable because he combines things contradictory; or a supreme power above God; or two
equal Gods. None of these three conclusions can be
accepted, because it is simply impossible to exercise
that trust, which is the Christian's high privilege, in
a God whom we have to conceive under one of these
three forms.

Opposed to this representation of God, which
makes justice his fundamental quality, is the conception of him as mere arbitrary will. It was first
set forth in the thirteenth century by Duns Scotus
Erigena, was in later times taken up by the Socinians
and became current among them and the Arminians
in variously modified forms. God is mere will—
"dominium absolutum." We can assign no reason
why he should act in one way rather than in another.

The laws of morality, such as we know them, are founded upon his caprice; he might just as well have reversed the value of right and wrong. Right is right for no other reason than that God has so willed it, and there is no reason why he should have so willed. He might have created the world differently. He is man's absolute master. We are his slaves. He can do with us as he chooses. If he deals with us according to a law, that is his choice. He might have made any other conceivable law and applied it to us. Why he placed us under the moral law as we know it, we cannot tell. It was his arbitrary will. In the fulness of his power he instituted the ordinance by which our relation to him is determined according to certain principles. God is not obliged to punish sin, he may freely forgive. He might have chosen some other way of redeeming man than through Christ. Everything is accidental; nothing is but might have been otherwise.

It is evident that the controlling influence in the formation of this conception was the desire to avoid the stumbling-block of the other theory, the assumption of a dualism in God. But the Scotian doctrine cannot be considered as marking an advance in theology. For, aside from the question how we can conceive of a being who is nothing but undetermined will, it is plain that a God whose essential characteristic is indifference falls behind the demands of the ethical and spiritual nature and therefore fails to satisfy the tests we recognise. The mere caprice of a God who is fundamentally indifferent to the distinctions of right and wrong is an insufficient basis for the ethical law. And how can we trust a God who has no feeling for us, who may annihilate us just as well as he may save us, and that for the same reason, namely —no reason? The appropriate feeling toward such a God would be the fear of the slave, not the confidence of the child.

The Scotian representation of God has to-day more of a theoretical than a practical interest. It stands aside from the great stream of theological thought. But it was necessary to thus briefly allude to it, in order to give completeness to our survey and to show that within the traditional limits of theological thought both alternatives are impossible.

Two conditions seem to require fulfilment before we can promise ourselves any adequate solution of the problem of God. The first is a more distinct recognition of the limits of human knowledge, the other is a more complete and candid examination of the data of revelation. These two conditions correspond to two branches of research in which there has been the greatest advance in modern times. The one department of philosophy in which we see with greater clearness, is that which deals with the nature of human faculties and their limits; while biblical criticism has placed the Bible in a new light and taught us to appreciate the meaning of revelation as never before.

We now understand that it is necessary to exercise self-restraint in our efforts to know God. The theological labours of past generations represent many futile attempts to transcend the limits of the finite. The terminology which was used, by its vagueness deceived those who used it into thinking that they had accomplished the impossible. So, when it was laid down that God was "pure being," "the ″Ον,"or " the absolute," or when God was defined as pure will. These terms, if they conveyed any meaning to the mind, conveyed it most indistinctly, but that very indistinctness was thought to be a mark of the infinite. The phantom, which was forever evading human grasp, was pursued with unabated eagerness, until at last it came to be recognised that there is a line drawn beyond which the human mind cannot go; on the other side is the unknowable, that which it is above our powers to comprehend. Life we may know, we may conceive of a being who represents life such as we know it in its fulness; but the grounds of this life, what it is in its essential nature: this is a secret which shall not be revealed until we are gifted with higher intelligence. And it avails nothing to invent terms and phrases which fail to explain, but, in reality, merely serve to state the problem.

The other condition is a clearer appreciation of the data of revelation. The one greatest effect of concentrating the labour of the keenest intellects upon the biblical problem, as has been done now for many years, is this: it has brought out Christ as the essential revelation of God. The Bible is no longer placed above Christ as an oracle of equal authority in all its parts, in any portion of which we may find equally valid elements of revelation. We recognise gradations in the Bible, and high above the book stands the life of Christ as revealing God. We find God in Christ. The story of his life, his deeds, his consciousness as his words reveal it, his mission as he himself conceived it and as it was received in the religious consciousness of his immediate followers: these are the data for our knowledge of God, and not the stories of Hebrew Judges, or a passage in a New Testament epistle of uncertain authorship.'

[1] Heb. xii. 29.

CHAPTER V.

THE IDEA OF GOD (*Continued*).

UNDERLYING the argumentation in this essay is the principle of the essential difference between metaphysical and religious thought. It comes especially into play in our reasoning about the idea of God; and as it is of fundamental importance to our purpose, I shall here pause in the argument in order to examine with some care into the nature and grounds of this principle and the limits of its application.

The first point in this examination must be an accurate definition of the terms used; they are two: first, Metaphysics; second, Religion. Metaphysics is that science which investigates the grounds of all being. The most ordinary observation soon learns to know the lack of reality in those things which come under our perception. There is no colour without the eye, no sound without the ear, no feeling without the touch. Hence the word "phenomenon" —that which appears; and we ask what is the reality underneath? The human mind knows nothing but phenomena. Matter, time, space; the forms of mental judgment, causation, possibility, necessity: all these are phenomena. Metaphysics asks, what is the reality underlying these phenomena?

In putting this question, metaphysics makes no distinction. It knows no differences of value. Spirit and matter are, in the eyes of the metaphysician, perfectly equal. They are both, alike, manifestations of a something behind. It is that something behind, which he is after. He is impartial; everything that comes under his observation is subjected to the same treatment. The one and only motive which he obeys is an insatiable curiosity to know, to penetrate as far as human intelligence can go.

It is at this point that we begin our differentiation of religion from metaphysics. The view of the world which presents itself to the eye of religion is not homogeneous. The world presents to religion an inveterate contradiction. That contradiction is the starting-point of the religious view of the world. It is the contradiction of matter and spirit, coming to a point in the nature of man. To the theologian this is the one fact of absorbing interest. I know myself to be an insignificant particle in the vast whole which we call Nature; I am one small factor in the grand comprehensive system of world-evolution. But do I, therefore, resign myself to being merely a part of a machine? The very fact that I am able to put the question carries with it a decided negative. I am told that I am descended from the lower animals, and that I am on a level with them. But when I want to know myself, I ask the man that I am, not the ape that I was. There is a voice within tells me with an irresistibly coercive force of argument that I and nature are not one, that there is in me something above nature. To vary a little the fine phrase which I have quoted from Mr. James Martineau, it is the irresistible pleading of personality that makes us rebel against confounding the "I" with nature.

This, then, is the fundamental difference between religion and metaphysics. To the eye of the metaphysician nature is one. To the eye of the theologian nature is two: my nature and nature outside of me.

From this initial distinction between the two we now proceed to differentiate the purposes which metaphysics and religion severally serve, and the ends which they aim at. I have already spoken of the motive which the metaphysician obeys: it is curiosity, that peculiar characteristic stamped upon the human mind, by which it is impelled to search through the heights and in the depths for the meaning of all things. The motive underlying religion springs from that contradiction of which I have spoken.

Religious beliefs have developed. The religious instincts have remained essentially the same from the beginning. Men have been led to religion by the same religious needs. The historical method of dealing with religion, which in other respects has been so sadly abused, informs us as to the religious instincts of the race. The religious want of man has always been that of a power above himself to help him against opposing forces, to furnish him the solution of the great contradiction of his nature. What conceptions have been held of that power, whether it was thought of as a ghost, an angel, or a god, makes no difference. The essential purpose which religious observances of any kind served was to find protection and aid against the powers of nature: disease, enemies, the elements. In this respect man has not changed. Here we have a characteristic inherent in human nature, the desire for help. As civilisation has advanced, the ideas of the nature of the protecting power and of the manner of its operation have become refined. But essentially, what the Christian seeks in his religion is the same as that which the original savage sought: the aid of a power above for the upholding of the claims of his personality as against the opposing forces of the world.

It is clear, therefore, that as the initial view of religion differs from that of the metaphysician, so the motive and the object differ. Religion is not prompted by curiosity. The motive behind religious observances and religious thought is as practical as that of the drowning man who reaches out for the plank to keep him above water. The object of religion is not to penetrate into the reality of the " thing in itself," but to make life worth living by opening up a vista of confidence and hope, to give the answer to the yearning of the heart which is so much deeper than the desire for knowledge: " Oh Lord, in thee have I trusted: let me never be confounded."

These considerations will go to explain why the god of metaphysics, if the metaphysical abstraction can be called a god, falls so far short of the fulness of the Christian idea of God. The god who is merely the substratum of reality underlying phenomena is very far from the being whom we seek that we may trust him. But the contrast which I have here drawn between the metaphysical and the religious must not be understood to imply that theology absolutely excludes the use of metaphysics. It will, therefore, now be necessary to state with all possible accuracy just what is claimed and what is denied.

We are always running up against this difficulty in religion, that when a principle is enunciated, especially if it is a new one, it is very apt to be taken hold of and set up as exclusive of all other principles. It is a popular tendency to judge by contraries. A thing must be either absolutely right or absolutely wrong. Our Saviour uttered certain rebukes against the abuse of riches. Riches were, therefore, to be condemned: hence asceticism. We find it hard to persuade men of the principle of proportion which Christ recognized. It is often not so much a question of what is absolutely right and what is absolutely wrong, as of what is first and what is second. So it is with our mental operations. We use our mind for the formation of different kinds of judgment. In every judgment, however, all the three psychical functions are operative: the intellect, the feeling, and the will. The judgments do not differ by the exclusion of any one of these functions; but they are distinguished by the prominence of the one or the other. In the theoretical judgments which are applied to the scientific investigation of phenomena, all three functions operate; but the intellectual is the dominant function. In the religious judgment the factor of feeling is the decisive one; but that does not imply that the intellectual is excluded.

This will help us to understand in how far religion excludes metaphysics. The former is governed by an intellectual interest in the grounds of all being. This interest is not entirely excluded from religion, but it is altogether subordinated to the practical interests of life. The religious judgments may be permeated by a metaphysical interest, but this interest is not the dominant factor. Religious thought is distinguished by the fact that the ultimate motive is always a practical one. The decisive factor in theological reasoning is the nearer or more remote value which the object has for the personal life.

The latter distinction between a nearer and more remote value leads us to a second qualification of the general contrast between metaphysics and religion. A religious judgment may be pursued to its consequences and become more and more metaphysical. We shall see, in the course of our further argument on the idea of God, that this idea is first reached by a strictly religious judgment. We learn to know first, not God in general, but our God, God so far as he has meaning and value for the ends of our personal life. But the idea of God being thus determined, the inquisitive functions of the mind impel us to go further and to harmonise this idea with other general notions. Our conception of God becomes thus more and more detached from actual experience. Nevertheless, the chain is not broken which binds the conception of God to the practical needs of life; we are only tracing it backward. This procedure, which begins with experience, with the God for us, and goes back step by step towards a knowledge of God in himself, is the reverse of that process which begins as far as possible from our personal needs in the barren abstraction of the Infinite or the Absolute, and upon that foundation builds the distinctively personal attributes of God.

I believe it is the one contribution to theology which more than any other will secure to Albrecht Ritschl a unique place among Christian thinkers, to have clearly defined the difference between metaphysical and religious thought. The consequences, I cannot but think, are very far-reaching. It may seem to some a mere academic distinction; but such forget that what is a distinct, tangible conception in the minds of the thoughtful is, in the minds of the great bulk of people, a habit of mind, a temper, a disposition, a way of looking at things. And, by the reverse process of reasoning, if any such habit of mind, temper, disposition, and way of looking at things in the common mind is held to be wrong and dangerous, the only way to change it is by tracing it to its logical antecedents and bringing convincing proof of the inadequacy of the corresponding form of thought as it is held by thinking minds.

There is a certain habit of mind and way of looking at religion widely current among the masses of the people, which is endangering the interests of religion. I appeal to those who have had the practical experience of the cure of souls. What is the greatest difficulty you have had to deal with? Is it not the inveterate tendency to confound curiosity with the religious instinct? Religion is made synonymous with the mere knowledge of supernatural things. Those who are excessively inquisitive about the time of Christ's second coming, the nature of the resurrection body, the millennial kingdom and all the many questions concerning the future life, will be utterly indifferent to the ethical and spiritual interests of religion. But this is simply the metaphysical curiosity of uninstructed minds.

A greater danger than this lies in the religious indifference and agnosticism of the cultured classes. Men of our generation are devoting an unparalleled enthusiasm to the ethical interests of humanity; but underneath this ethical enthusiasm there is, we cannot deny it, an indifference to, and a suspicion of, the strictly religious, which as surely as all action must proceed from conviction, will yield a disastrous harvest in the coming generation. And why this indifference, this suspicion? Simply because educated men are no longer interested in truths which have been presented to them as intellectual verities; simply because our theology has not shown the connection between the sacred truths of religion and the practical necessities of everyday life.

If we are ever to have a revival of true religion, if men shall come again to view life in the light of the revelation of Jesus, the first condition is that the metaphysical canker be cut out of religion and the spiritual interests of man be once more acknowledged in their supreme importance.

I have said that two things are necessary before we can hope to solve the problem of God: the recognition of the limitations imposed upon human knowledge, and a better understanding of the revelation of God in Christ. Recalling to our minds these necessary conditions, we now proceed to enquire into the nature of the Christian idea of God.

At the opening of our Morning Prayer there is an expression, significant from the position in which it stands, which points to the true knowledge of God in Christ. When, in the general confession, we have confessed our sins, the priest stands up to " declare and pronounce to his people, being penitent, the Absolution and Remission of their sins," and he does this in the name of "*Almighty God, the Father of our Lord Jesus Christ.*" The Church bids us seek forgiveness of the God who is " the Father of our Lord Jesus Christ." With a true insight, the Church recognises in the expression of God's relation to Christ the revelation to the Christian of the true nature of God. He is a God of love.

We distinguish several elements in Christ's revelation. There is first the bare fact of his having been sent into the world. There was strongly impressed upon Christ the sense of his mission; hence his frequent references to being " sent ": " That the world may know that thou *hast sent me*." His followers distinctly received him as sent from heaven for the benefit of man: " This is a true saying and worthy of all men to be received that Christ Jesus came into the world to save sinners " (1 Tim. i. 15); " We have seen and do testify that the Father sent the Son to be the Saviour of the world " (1 John iv. 14). Christ came as from God and was received as the gift of God. And when those who thus received him reflected upon the nature of the God who had sent Christ, there could be but one conclusion. This conclusion is distinctly expressed by St. John (1, iv. 9): " In this was manifested the love of God toward us, because that God sent his only-begotten Son into the world, that we might live through him." This is a clear statement of the impression which the mission of Christ makes in regard to the nature of God. The God who sent his Son into the world to save man is a God of love. The simple fact of Christ's mission can be interpreted in no other way. It could have proceeded but from one motive: love. This is the primary revelation of God which we have in Christ.

Then there is the teaching of Christ. Where are the essential points of Christ's teaching to be found ? In the appendix to some parables, in language which is strongly figurative, which speaks of the fire that is not quenched and the worm which dieth not ? Or shall we turn to find the burden of Christ's teaching to such chapters as the fifteenth of St. Luke, with its parables of the lost sheep, the lost coin, and the prodigal son? and to the last chapters of St. John's Gospel, the instructions to the disciples at the last supper and the high-priestly prayer? Surely the candid student of Christ's words must admit that if there was one truth above all others that Christ sought to impress, it was a heavenly Father's love.

Finally, there are Christ's actions. These speak with no uncertain sound. St. Peter sums up his activity in these words: " He went about doing good." It is only that dualistic conception which separates love and justice, Christ and the Father, that can fail to recognise in the beneficent activity of Christ—an activity which had but one purpose, that of bringing happiness to man—the revelation of a God to whom the well-being of his children is the supreme purpose, who, therefore, is a God of love.

If we take Christ in his earthly life as the revelation of God, we cannot fail to acknowledge as the Christian idea of God, a God whose nature is love.[1]

[1] There is no sharper antithesis in theology than between that doctrine which begins with God and goes on to Christ, and that which begins with Christ and leads up to God the Father. The theology which begins with the Christian God as given (by reason or by nature) has but an accidental place for Christ. The permanent and necessary place of Christ in theology is as the revelation of God, the means of knowing God: "He that hath seen me hath seen the Father." I may refer to Browning's "Epistle of Karshish" for a most powerful and striking presentation of this significance of Christ.

But it will be maintained that there are other attributes which must be added before God's full nature has been expressed; that alongside of the love there is something else; that there is, in short, another side of God's nature. There is the holiness of God, his righteousness, his justice, his anger; all these are plainly stamped upon the Bible's revelation of God. And not only does the Old Testament teach them, but the New Testament, though it does not give to these attributes the same prominence, yet does acknowledge their presence in God. Let us, therefore, consider these qualities.

Holiness is the fundamental character of God in the Old Testament. "I the Lord your God am holy" (Lev. xix. 2)—these words express the thought of an Hebrew. In the New Testament this quality gives way to another and is almost lost out of sight. Holiness is not like the other attributes of God, a single quality; it is rather a comprehensive characterisation. It filled out the Hebrew's entire conception of Jehovah. Its principal notes are: first, unapproachableness. This meaning carries with it the distinction of God from man, his distance above the sphere of the human. Secondly, it expresses God's aversion to impurity. It is the contrary of sin. The holiness of God is therefore understood as denoting the negation of those imperfections which attach to the creature. As such it is an essential element in our idea of God. God is to us a holy God. But we must be careful not to apply this character to God as he is prior to his relation to man. As forming a background to the character of God, holiness has no meaning; for it becomes intelligible only by its negation, sin, and sin has no place in God's being. Therefore God's holiness forms no opposition to his love. His holiness is known to us only in his love, not as a quality apart from his love. God is not known to us as first holy, then loving; but only as holy love. When we say that God is love, we mean that there is nothing behind his love, no other quality of which we become cognisant as antecedent to his love. We must, it is true, conceive of God as omnipotent and omniscient, but he is all-powerful and all-wise in his love. So, also, he is holy; but we learn to know him as holy in his love.

In speaking of the atonement, I endeavoured to show that the forgiveness of sins can rightly be referred only to God as Father. It is the fault of the popular theory that it starts from the necessity of a satisfaction to God before man can be forgiven. This leads inevitably to that dualism in our conception of God in which it is impossible for the mind to rest. The simple representation of God, as it is given to us in the revelation of Christ, does away with the dualism. The necessity of the satisfaction which Christ wrought was in man. God did not have to be reconciled. There is nothing in God behind his holy love which stands in the way of his free forgiveness.

We see then how the idea of God is the touchstone of our theories of the atonement. A false theory leads to a false conception of God. On the other hand, the theory of the atonement which I have endeavoured to set forth leads to a conception of God which is at one in itself, in which the mind finds rest.

There is but a shade of difference between the attribute of holiness as applied to God, and those of righteousness and justice. As the background of his being, as the groundwork of his character, they are alike inconceivable. The attribute of justice, under another meaning, that of the equal treatment of all, follows from his love. For it is evident that God must treat all alike if he loves his creatures.

It remains to deal with the last objection that has been mentioned. What about the wrath of God? God's wrath appears indelibly stamped upon the Bible and seems necessary to an adequate conception of the Deity. Just here, however, we are impressed with the great distance that separates the Old Testament from the New. The former is full of wrath and vengeance; and if we had to consider the Old Testament as God's supreme revelation to man and were not obliged to allow for a very decided anthropomorphic tendency, we should have to revise very considerably the foregoing statements in regard to the being of God. But we find that the wrath of God is by no means wanting in the New Testament and in the words of Christ. A brief examination of these passages will be necessary.

Where the wrath of God is expressed in the gospels, it is directed against hardened sinners. So it is at the conclusion of the various eschatological parables, as the parable of the feast: "Bind him hand and foot, and take him away and cast him into outer darkness; there shall be weeping and gnashing of teeth" (St. Matt. xxii. 13). We have also, as bearing upon this point, those scenes in which Christ's indignation comes out, as in the desecration of the temple and the denunciation of the Pharisees. Taking these several instances into consideration, we may draw this conclusion: there is a legitimate sense in which wrath can be predicated of God. It may mean, first, the final turning away of God from those who are hopelessly hardened in sin, who have taken the definitive resolve against the divine love. This seems to be the meaning in the parables. Then, there must be a place for God's wrath as against all persistent sin. Here it is the reverse of his love, the divine attitude as against sin. But here, again, we must carefully guard against that dualism which would conceive of God's wrath for his own sake. Vengeance is a decidedly anthropomorphic term applied to God. If we allow any idea of vindictiveness, any notion that God inflicts suffering for the sake of satisfying a supposed "righteousness" in himself, we set up a god above our God, and make him unthinkable. So too with God's punishment. We may conceive of physical evil or of the distress of conscience as the punishment of sin, but not as inflicted by God to gratify himself; rather as a means of correcting and training his creatures. So understood, punishment flows from God's love.

We may illustrate the limits within which we can conceive of the wrath or the punishment of God by the analogy which Christ most frequently used, that of father. We generally account it a sign of weakness when a father loses his temper in punishing a child. He then does it out of vindictiveness. But a father rightly punishes out of love for the child, to improve its character. So, too, a father, after he has done all he could for his child, and the child persistently turns from him and perseveres in his evil course and hardens himself to all loving appeals, may give way to his indignation, may utter scathing rebuke, and in the end may turn from the child and cut off all intercourse with him. He will be henceforth a stranger. But is not this indignation and the final sentence perfectly in accord with a father's love? Can we not imagine, even while the father's indignation is kindling his tongue to the sharpest rebuke, that his heart is wrung with anguish for the waywardness of the loved child? and even when he turns from him, after all effort has proved futile, it is in deepest sorrow; and if the child should show at any moment signs of repentance, would not the father—as Christ described it in the parable—quickly go to meet him?

"It is of the greatest importance for a systematic method of theology, that we should never leave out of view the divergence between our individual religious reflexion and the form of theological speculation 'sub specie æternitatis.'" The distinction, which this quotation from Ritschl makes, is between the feeling which comes to us naturally according to the anthropomorphic way of thinking of God, and the higher conceptions which we form, when we subject our natural impressions to the control of reason and try to harmonise our ideas. It is natural that we should in a devotional attitude feel the "wrath" of God, and natural that we should pray, as we do in the Litany and elsewhere, to be delivered from his wrath; but in our reflective moments we correct and give the proper interpretation to the anthropomorphism contained in such forms.

We conclude, therefore, that the wrath of God, properly understood, does not demand any other conception of God than that of holy love. One important practical corollary is to be drawn from this conclusion. It applies to the use of fear in religion. The appeal to the sense of fear in the unconverted is based upon a different conception of God than that above given. The latter allows no scope to fear, as commonly understood, in the Christian religion. The "fear of God" is a different thing from the trembling before the vindictive, vengeful being, who in the minds of many has stood in the place of God. It is quite certain that the appeal to fear, by placing before men such a God in place of " the Father of our Lord Jesus Christ," will not result in that sense of religion which Christ sought to awaken. If there is any scope for fear in Christianity, it is the fear which is excited in the wrongdoer when his eyes are opened to see where his course is leading him—the fear of becoming what he now recognises as an awful possibility. This fear may become a motive to a better life; but such fear is only awakened when one has experienced the love of God.

It is a fault of our theology that it does not enquire into the nature of God's love, and that the term is supposed to carry with it nothing more than the emotional sentiment which we are accustomed to associate with affection. And yet the nature of God's love yields to analysis. Here, again, the analogy of human fatherhood holds. As a father's love is something more than a mere effusion of sentiment, so is God's; and a juster appreciation of the true quality of God's love will throw a flood of light upon the central doctrine of Christian theology. First, then, we find that God's love involves the singling out of the individual, the recognition of each in the rights of his personality. To believe in God's love means primarily to believe that I am not lost in an indistinguishable mass of humanity, but that God has singled me out, that God's eye is ever upon me, that my individual life has, in his sight, its own value. But it means more than this: it means that God sees me not only as I am, but also as I may be, not only the actuality, but also the possibility, and that he longs to make that possibility real. He recognises the purpose and the ideal of each man's life, and that purpose and ideal he has taken up into his own thought and purpose. To have learned to know myself the object of God's love, to have become conscious of the divine eye singling me out and resting upon me, and to have awakened to the fact that God looks upon me not only as I am, but also as I may be, that God is ever comparing me with my ideal: what stronger motive could ever come into the life of man than this? Could any representation of future judgment have softened the heart of Zacchaeus as did the sudden revelation flashed into his soul when Jesus singled him out in the crowd, that even he, the outcast among men, was an object of care and love to Jesus? How different the idea he must from that moment have had of his own life, of his value before God. This is the motive that Christianity brings into the life of man: the appreciation of his own humanity. It was well said by one of the writers of *Lux Mundi*, that man to be saved must know not only that he cannot save himself, but " how splendidly worth saving he was."¹ To know this; to understand that before the almighty Creator and Sustainer of the world I stand in the dignity of my personality, that he recognises the rights that belong to me as one created in the likeness of himself, that God has placed before me possibilities for infinite good; to have the eyes to see my own ideal as the divinely appointed " might be " of my life: this is to know the love of God, and this is Christ's motive to a better life.

It may be said that this motive is too high for hardened sinners, that they need a rougher treatment to rouse them to a sense of sin. Christ, when

¹ " The Preparation in History for Christ."

he found them desecrating the temple, did not talk to those men about a beautiful ideal. He made a scourge of cords and drove them out. True. But was it fear that made those men go quietly trooping out of the sacred precincts, driven by one man? Not fear, but shame. It was because Christ had awakened in them a sense of the unworthiness of their action, that they did what no mere fear would have made them do. Shame is the sense of the incongruity of our actions with that personal worth which is ours as the objects of God's love. The sense of shame comes often as the first step towards a better life. The first suggestion rising in the mind of what I ought to be, of what God wills me to be, awakens the feeling of shame. I begin to look with suspicion, then with dislike, finally with aversion and horror, upon what I have done. I learn to know that I have injured myself. A new feeling is awakened—the respect of self. As I grow in knowledge of my better self, I shrink more and more from my former self. And so I learn to value myself as God values me, and to know and aspire to the life which God has appointed for me. And while this feeling is being intensified, it becomes every day more clear to me what the love of God means. So, all through the process, from the beginning to the end, it is the same divine love, first awakening the sense of shame—not, perhaps, without a rough shaking—and then quickening into life the dormant aspirations. In the gospels we look in vain for any appeal to fear that Christ made. Even the betrayal of Peter called from him only the rebuke of a glance; but that glance was enough to bring an agony of shame into Peter's heart, so that he went from Christ's presence and wept bitterly.

As soon as the sinner turns to God, he feels the divine love whose arms are ever open to receive him back. All fear, that is incompatible with this love of God, such as has been appealed to (more in the past than in the present) as a religious motive, such as to-day in the Roman Catholic Church forms the basis of a huge ramified system of compromises with an angry God: all such fear we, if we follow the teachings of Jesus, must rule out of the Christian system.

We conclude, therefore, in opposition to that theory which makes righteousness the fundamental attribute of God, and to that which represents him as mere arbitrary will, that God is to be conceived as love. You think of God as love or you do not think of him at all. You think nothing in God before his love. Holy love is the all-sufficient conception of God.

I have omitted one factor in the idea of God which has played an important part in theological systems: personality. I shall do no more than glance at it, because I cannot bring myself to think that it is of any practical importance. The denial of God's personality, according to the well-known aphorism of Spinoza " Omnis determinatio est negatio," is one of those metaphysical subtleties which have done much to confuse theological thought. Mr. John Fiske in his *Idea of God*, says (p. 135) that " to ascribe what we know as human personality to the infinite Deity straightway lands us in a contradiction, since personality without limits is inconceivable." But inasmuch as the human mind is incapable of conceiving anything without limits, as, in fact, the nature of the infinite is utterly and entirely outside of the sphere of possible human knowledge, it is difficult to see what force there is in this objection. Personality being the highest conception of spiritual power which the human mind can form, the conclusion is irresistible that the mind would stultify itself if it did not ascribe to the creator at least the perfection of the creature. Mr. Fiske does attribute "a quasi-psychical nature" to the Deity and this would seem to be very much the nature under which any thoughtful Christian conceives God.[1]

We have, therefore, nothing to add to our definition: God is holy love. This is the only conception of the Supreme Being in which the mind comes to rest. But we must go one step further. Love is inconceivable without an object, just as pure will without an object of the will cannot be imagined. If, therefore, God is love, there must be an object of God's love. This object of God's love is the kingdom of God.

[1] It is doubtless true, as Mr. Spencer points out, that we cannot imagine the Supreme Being as possessed with attributes proper to humanity, such as consciousness, will, intelligence. But can we not, and must we not, believe the perfection of the Deity to involve all the highest attributes of humanity? Otherwise we stultify ourselves with this absurdity, that the universe, including man, proceeds from a being who is in his nature lower than his works.

Here we come upon that historic phenomenon which we set out to investigate. We found that Christ came to establish the kingdom of God. Certain words of Christ led us to the recognition of a religious determination of life within that kingdom. We have followed the various steps of that process, from sin to forgiveness, and through forgiveness to the eternal life, and that brought us to consider the idea of God, in which all true thought of the Christian life must centre. And now we are brought to this conclusion: that the true conception of God as the God of love must recognise as the object of his love that kingdom of God which Christ came to earth to establish. This completes our idea of God.

The love of God for the kingdom of God means that he takes up the end and purpose of that organisation of men into his own thought and purpose. He makes its end and object his own. We think of God as love because we think of him as setting before himself as his object, end, and purpose, the building up of the human race into the kingdom of God. Here we get a glimpse of God's comprehensive plan. We see the kingdom of God in its inception eighteen hundred years ago. Christ even then comprehended its destination; from the little seed it was to grow into a great tree overshadowing the earth. And looking back we can see how this destination has been in the process of realisation. It has been a slow process, but the principle of expansion has never staid its work. We know not by what steps the future will advance towards a fuller realisation of that kingdom, but we do know that this kingdom of God is the key to human history. The destiny of the world is bound up with it. It has in the very being of God the assurance of ultimate triumph. For to us God becomes intelligible only as we conceive his love to have taken the kingdom of God up into his own purpose. In the light of this great truth we can see how all tends to the advancement of this kingdom of God. The material world becomes a minister to the spiritual world; the creation below man serves the purposes of man, and all the countless forms of matter adapted to the use and gratification of man, exist for the kingdom of God, as a means of its realisation.

But, one may ask, what of the time before there was any kingdom of God, before there was any world? It might be objected that the kingdom of God, being temporal and still in the process of realisation and, therefore, contingent, is not fitted to be the object of the divine love. If God in his essential nature is love and we cannot conceive of love without an object, the object of God's love must be commensurate with his being, it must be eternal.

This question brings us to the borderland of the unknowable. We stand as it were on the shore of a vast ocean. We strain our eyes to catch a glimpse of something beyond. We have some faint suggestions of a farther shore; driftwood is cast upon our strand; the winds carry the fragrance of another continent; and such indications allow us to guess at the nature of the strange land. So it is with our thoughts of heaven and of God. As far as we need a God as an object of trust we can know him; but when the mind pries further and seeks to know him as he is, it can only reason, cautiously and timidly, from the indications we have to what seem their necessary conditions. We know God to be love, we believe the object of his love to be his kingdom. But the farther we proceed in our search into the nature of God, the more slender grows the thread which connects our speculations with the concrete facts of experience.

Bearing in mind this caution we may say in answer to the difficulty suggested, that for us the kingdom of God is indeed an event in time; it had a beginning and will have a consummation in time. But as far as we can understand what time is, we must conceive it as a subjective condition of our knowledge, something inherent in us as finite creatures. And, although God must stand in some relation to time, yet there is a sense in which God stands above time. " Eternity," says Ritschl, " is the power of the spirit over time." As such, we ourselves have a certain experience of eternity. We must think of God as free from the limitations of time. The conditions of time in the realisation of his kingdom do not exist for him. The kingdom of God, in its full consummation, is from eternity the object of the divine contemplation; the perfect realisation of that kingdom is an ever-present experience with God. And, therefore, the kingdom of God is an object commensurate to the love of God.

Another reflection will perhaps serve to supplement this train of thought, or may be a substitute for the conception of the eternal significance of the kingdom of God for God. We have seen that Christ is the type of that relationship into which God entered with his followers, that is, with his kingdom. The love of God for his kingdom is prefigured by the love of God for Christ. If we conceive Christ, according to the doctrine of the Church, as the second person of the Trinity, the love of God for his kingdom finds its eternal type in the love of the Father for the eternally begotten Son. Then the kingdom of God and Christ are correlated conceptions. Then the life of the kingdom of God is a part of the divine life thrown out from God, and for reasons utterly beyond our ken subjected to the conditions of time and space and so entering into the historic relationships familiar to us.

We are conscious of the weakness of our wings as we try to soar above the sphere of experience into the realm of pure realities. But the mind cannot abnegate an imperious instinct to probe its own conceptions to the very last consequences. Harm is done when these speculations are raised to the dignity of finality and receive the imprimatur of Christian doctrine.

We come back to this: the Christian faith demands that we conceive God as one, and that unity can only be love. We do not think God at all unless we think him in relation to his kingdom as seeking the realisation of that kingdom's end and object. The idea of God as a God of love for his kingdom is such that the Christian mind can find rest in it, as will be seen if we apply to it our ethical and spiritual tests. First, this idea satisfies the ethical demands of our nature. It avoids the difficulties of both the other theories; it neither assumes a necessity above God as the seat of the moral law, nor does it make the moral law subject to the arbitrary will of God. According to our theory, goodness is inherent in the nature of God. For God and the kingdom of God are inseparably connected. God, in his self-determination, determines himself with reference to the kingdom of God; and as we found the kingdom of God to be, either in itself or in its type, the eternal object of God's love, it follows that there never was a time when his will did not realise itself for the good of this kingdom; that is, it works from eternity in the manner which we, from our point of view, call the laws of goodness. These laws, therefore, have their seat in God's nature, in such manner that they neither stand above God nor are the creatures of his caprice. Thus the ethical demands of our nature are satisfied.

Our spiritual craving also receives satisfaction. The God whom we think of only as a God of love is one whom we can trust. The heart comes to rest, we are satisfied with such a God. We do not want to stand in dread of our God, and we need not. The God of whom I think as the father in the parable, or as the shepherd in the other story, allows me to look up to him as a child to his father, as

Christ did. This is the God who makes men brave, the God who makes us feel that the world is of little account with him on our side.

The essential difference between this and the dualistic idea of God is that the latter assumes an end and purpose for which God exists other than the world. God lives for his own glory, his own honour. Hence the fatal dualism. Our view identifies the purpose of God and the purpose for which the world exists. We have seen that God's love means the taking up of the final end of the kingdom of God into his own thought and purpose. Hence, the two coincide, are identical. The consummation of human society according to the eternal laws of right: this is the end and object of God's kingdom. It is also God's own eternal purpose. And therefore the progressive realisation of the kingdom of God upon earth is a fuller and fuller revelation of the nature of God.

This truth of the unity of purpose of God and the world affords the final solution of the problem of the freedom of the will. Two seemingly contradictory truths are postulated by religion: man's dependence upon God and the freedom of the will.

The idea of the freedom of the will has been scouted as an absurdity.[1] But we may still be allowed to hold that there is a difference between the acts of volition in man and those of the brute. That every act of the will has behind it a motive,

---

[1] Compare John Fiske, *Cosmic Philosophy*.

goes without saying. The will obeys the strongest motive; this motive exists in the shape of feeling. But what determines the feeling? This is the point at which the enquiry into the freedom of the will must begin.

The freedom of the will rests upon the power of the reason, the ability to balance motives. The brute obeys only the brute instinct. That is the lowest motive. Above that of the brute instinct is the stage of a calculating selfishness. Then there is the stage where the motives are subservient to family relationship. That is the first step on the ladder of civilisation. Above that is the stage where the motives of conduct are under tribal or national influence. Patriotism is the mark of a highly evolved ethical system. But it is not the highest. In the highest stage the motives of action are brought under subserviency to the end for which man was created—the kingdom of God. It is only when we recognise the motives which are correlated to the kingdom of God as those which rightly govern man's actions, that we understand what the freedom of the will is. Only when man has raised himself to the plane upon which his conduct is governed by reason, or—which is the same thing—by considerations of the ultimate end and purpose of his life, is there freedom of choice. Every other set of motives, that of the animal instincts, of calculating selfishness, of family or national interests, involves a certain amount of limitation, a certain bondage of the will. The will must act in obedience to the most comprehensive human motive, to be really free. This is the motive corresponding to the laws of the kingdom of God. The freedom of the will may therefore be defined as the self-determination of man according to the laws of the kingdom of God.

But, as we have seen, this same kingdom of God is the object of God's love. The end of the kingdom of God is God's own eternal purpose. It is God's object to effect the realisation of the kingdom of God by the same laws in obedience to which man experiences freedom. God's law is the sphere of man's liberty. God's law is our " law of liberty." I exercise freedom of will by the determination of my conduct in accordance with the laws which represent God's own purpose for me. Therefore, in obeying God's law I am free, at the same time that I feel my dependence upon God. The apparent paradox is a fact of daily experience. The problem is solved when we recognise the identity of purpose between God and man.

We began this enquiry into the idea of God by asking what nature had to teach us. We found that, with the exception of one delicate hint which beauty in nature gives, it brings before us rather a God who is cruel and regardless of the well-being of his creatures. We then examined the Christian idea of God. We had to reject certain current ideas; but we found that the conception of the Supreme Being which is revealed to us in the gospels satisfies those tests by which we must judge, the demands of the ethical and of the spiritual nature. The moral nature and the spiritual nature cry out for a God, and the God revealed by Christ is the only God who satisfies their longing. The knowledge of " the Father of our Lord Jesus Christ " comes to us in answer to what the poet calls the

> " Vexing, forward reaching sense
> Of some more noble permanence."

Upon this foundation our belief in God stands firm: it is the meeting of the human aspirations and the revelation of Christ. The one is the answer to the other, and in this answer to human needs lies the strength of Christian conviction. But we should altogether fail to grasp the true significance of this Christian idea of God if we thought of it as one which we are merely permitted to hold. A good many people seem to think of religion very much as if the Christian were a sort of spoiled child, who has worried his parents into giving him a toy to play with. We are ever fearful lest some new attack upon religion may possibly rob us of our God. And so we hardly dare bring it out into the light of day; we cherish it in secret, lest it might catch the envious eye of some bold champion of that terrible bugbear of the modern Christian, " Science," and provoke him to the attack.

A little reflection will show that the foregoing train of thought carries with it not only the permission but the necessity of the Christian idea of God. Not only may we, as Christians, think of God as

Christ thought of him; but as thinking, reasoning beings we are obliged to assume the Christian idea of God. Consider: what takes place in every act of reflective thought? The astronomer makes his brain the centre from which he sweeps through the stellar universe; the chemist in his single person places himself over against the whole material world and it becomes the object of his analysis; the historian comprehends in his survey all life, past and present. Underlying these operations of the mind we are forced to recognise a fact of the utmost significance. This fact is the claim of superiority to nature which the human spirit makes. By nature is meant all that comes under the law of causation, including the phenomena of human life. The acts of conscious reflection which the astronomer, the chemist, the historian, and every other thinker performs are the assertion of a uniqueness belonging to the human spirit, of a right to set itself up against all the world. They are the manifestation of a distinguishing human faculty, the power to objectify the world. Recognising this uniqueness of the human spirit, we are obliged to take one of two alternatives. Either we must confess that we have no explanation of it. But the mind cannot rest in this agnosticism. It must go forward, if it is true to itself. Or we must acknowledge that the only adequate foundation for that claim of the individual human spirit is the Christian God, who as a God of love is to me the guarantee that the dignity which my personality claims for itself is founded in eternal truth.

On this ground, Ritschl criticises Strauss's well-known figure of the huge world-machine, with its iron teeth and hammers, to whose cruelty we are a helpless prey. Strauss comforts himself with the reflection that the machine has not only merciless wheels, but also soothing oil: this is the power of habit to alleviate suffering. Of this figure Ritschl says: either we are parts of the machine; then we can form no conception of the whole and its working; in that case we do not need any soothing oil, if when we are worn out we are replaced by new parts. Or else, men are distinguished from the machine as intelligent onlookers, at the same time that they are crushed by it: "Then, surely, it is no alleviation and no comfort to be sprayed with rancid oil; that is, by the persuasion of the inevitable necessity of their own destruction to be deprived of the consciousness of their own value which they drew from the fact that, because they were able to examine the machine and to have a knowledge of its construction, they were superior to it." The very effort, therefore, which the materialist makes to demonstrate that man is on the same plane with nature refutes his proposition. He could not make that effort did he not objectify nature. The very fact that he sets himself up as a critic of the world and of himself is possible only by the tacit assumption of a something in him which outranks the material universe, to whose level he seeks to degrade himself. The only adequate explanation, and therefore the only sufficient foundation, for the energetic self-determination of man by intellect and will is the God whose love for his children secures for them the full realisation of their destined place in the future, to which they have a right, but to which the weakness of their physical nature is a bar in the present.

With this we bring our argument for the idea of God to a conclusion. The conception of God which it has been attempted to establish differs in some important particulars from that which is officially held and taught. It does not, however, differ from the ideal which the pulpit of to-day very generally teaches. We must acknowledge a divergence between our practical teaching and our theoretical standards. Our theories are still held within the traditional bounds; the old formulas are still in vogue; we render them a formal homage, but that respect being paid we proceed to contradict our theory by our practice. A God who is primarily justice and righteousness is still the formal assumption; but we preach a God of love.

How much we have changed in this respect becomes impressively evident from a glance at such discourses as those of Jonathan Edwards. The most conservative theologian of to-day would turn with abhorrence from the kind of God depicted in sermons as that on "The justice of God in the damnation of sinners," or "Sinners in the hands of an angry God." A foot-note to the latter states that it was "attended with remarkable impressions on many of the hearers." We read the sermon and we are astonished. It would never enter into the mind of man to-day to make such an appeal in a Christian pulpit. That sort of teaching has passed away. The burden of Christian preaching to-day is a God of love.[1]

The comparison with Jonathan Edwards suggests another thought. Edwards, in his New England rural parish, in a community which Lowell said he believed was the most virtuous that ever existed, preached a God of terror. We, in our large cities, oppressed by a mass of wickedness such as Edwards never dreamt of, try to bring men to a consciousness of a God of love. Is it not because a deeper knowledge of human sin has given us a profounder appreciation of that love which never tires in its search for the sinner?

Experience, that best teacher of theology, has taught us to preach a God of love. The need of

[1] Nowhere probably can the monstrous results of pure theological intellectualism be seen so clearly as in Edwards. Compare such language as this: "The greater part of those who heretofore have lived under the same means of grace, and are now dead, are undoubtedly gone to hell." Also this: "All that preserves them every moment is the mere arbitrary will, and uncovenanted, unobliged forbearance, of an incensed God." (" Sinners in the hands of an angry God "). One has to read such discourses as these to understand how our conceptions of Christianity are altered. A study of mediæval art is also instructive in this respect. Take, for instance, Michael Angelo's *Last Judgment*. The attitude of Christ, the terror expressed in all faces, the entire absence of joy even among the redeemed, the exclusion of any suggestion of love; all this corresponds with the wrath and fear which the mind of the Middle Ages associated with the judgment. No modern painter would so paint it.

human nature has turned us from a cold intellectualism and has opened in the working Church a greater depth of insight to realise the balm she has to heal bleeding wounds, the food to still spiritual hunger. And she sets before men a God whom they can trust. But while she is doing this she still holds to the old theory which contradicts her present practice. While she tells men from the pulpit that God is a God of love, she teaches in her schools that God is a God of wrath.[1]

This alienation between practical and theoretical Christianity cannot but be disastrous in its consequences. A "practical Christianity" which has not under it a foundation of reasoned conviction is worth little more than any other groundless prejudice. The embers may glow on for a while, but they will soon die out.

It is not pretended that this presentation of the Christian idea of God satisfactorily solves every difficulty. But, founded as it is upon the revelation of Christ, it produces harmony in our thoughts and is fitted to form the groundwork of a strong conviction.

[1] "There is a reconciliation needed for which all devout and reverent men yearn, and it is the reconciliation between dogma and religion."—Ian Maclaren, *The Cure of Souls*, chap. v.

CHAPTER VI.

THE PERSON OF CHRIST.

WHEN Christian truth has been extricated from the mass of alien material with which metaphysical reasoning has encumbered it, it is found to be very simple. The salient points are: forgiveness, the eternal life, a God of love, the revelation of Christ. These are vital truths, upon which rest the hope, the comfort, the strength of religion. We have been trying to understand the connection and the harmony between them.

As we proceeded in our argument, we have been aware of the fact that our reasoning has been based upon an assumption which we have not verified, that there is a great underlying question which we have not answered. To that question we shall now return. It is the question of the authenticity of the gospels.

I wish here to recall what was said in the Introduction, that no proof, as commonly understood, would be attempted. The task of the theologian is to give an analysis of the Christian faith; the conviction of the truth must come from the answer which the facts of Christianity render to the religious needs of man. But it is necessary at this point to enquire whether the facts upon which Christian truth is based are trustworthy. We cannot neglect the historic basis of Christianity. Otherwise it would hang in the air. If there were no sufficient warrant for these vital truths in the facts of history, we should have to say: it is a very beautiful picture of the imagination, but it is a dream and nothing more. We cannot eliminate the historic element from Christianity. We must recognise the fact that Christianity enters into our lives through the means of certain actual facts of human experience.

The connecting link between our lives and the Christian truth is the historic Christ. The knowledge of Christ is a necessary factor in the Christian life. God has appointed him as the means to salvation, not because forgiveness must be wrung from an unwilling judge, but because man could not otherwise be brought back to the Father. Christ's influence upon man is twofold: first, he convinces man of sin; secondly, he brings forgiveness. This influence proceeds from the record of Christ's life; it touches us through the knowledge of that life as portrayed in the gospels. Untold multitudes have traced the principle of a new life in them to the knowledge of the life of Jesus. This fact alone raises a presumption in favour of the gospel records. Seeing, as we do, that Christ has come as a new leaven into the mass of humanity; understanding, as we do, that the life of Christian nations, in all its wonderful complexity, rests upon Christianity:— having before our minds the effect which the life of the one man, Jesus of Nazareth, has produced in the world, we are strongly disposed to accept the account of that life as true.

Nevertheless, should criticism succeed in proving that such a man as Jesus never lived, or that the record of his life is untrustworthy, we should be forced to reconstruct our theories. We cannot entirely spiritualise faith. It is futile to pretend that Christianity is quite independent of criticism. The Christian faith does depend upon certain facts of our knowledge. If there was no Christ, there can be no Christianity. It will, therefore, be necessary to take into consideration the grounds for believing in the historic character of Christ, and in doing so we are brought face to face with the immense labour which this and preceding generations have spent upon the problem.

It is far beyond the scope of this essay to present a history of modern criticism. It will be sufficient to indicate the drift of research in this department and to draw the limits of what we may look upon as settled.

There have been from the beginning critics of the Christian system. But not until towards the close of the last century did biblical criticism become more than the sporadic attempts of individual scholars. At that time it began to be a movement of the general religious mind. Since then it has gone through many phases. One theory after another has been propounded, enthusiastically received, and abandoned. So it was with the early rationalistic attempts to eliminate the supernatural and professedly to vindicate the character of Jesus as a great teacher. Then came the celebrated myth-theory of Strauss, and to many judgment seemed to have been pronounced upon Christianity. But time and the closer examination of the records proved this theory untenable, and it was succeeded by another.

Aside from the main stream of theological development stood the Frenchman Renan, who dissolved the story of Jesus into an oriental romance, and by the exquisite charm of his language captivated many. But who believes in Renan to-day?

Strauss and his myth-theory was succeeded by the Tübingen school with its most illustrious representative, the keen Baur, who explained Catholic Christianity as the compromise of two "tendencies," the Gentile and Jewish. This is the last theory. Baur's conception, elaborated by a host of able successors, for a long time fascinated Christian thinkers. Its influence has not yet altogether died out. But as a theory it has been given up. It has not stood the test of criticism.[1] The minute investigations into the text and history of the gospels have moved the dates of their composition so much higher up,

[1] "The magnificent attempt of Baur to explain Catholicism as a product of the opposition and the neutralisation of Jewish and Gentile Christianity (which Baur identifies with Paulinism) deals with two factors, of which one had no significance whatever and the other only an indirect significance for the formation of the Catholic Church."—Harnack, *Dogmengeschichte*, vol. i., page 277 (third edition).

that the theory of a prolonged conflict between two "tendencies" within the church antecedent to the writing of our present gospels must be abandoned.

In its turn the "tendency" theory has given place to another school. The day of "theories" is past. The present generation of scholars is devoting its energies to the critical investigation of the biblical records. The Tübingen school has been succeeded by the present "critical school."

It is to the labours of those who are subjecting the Christian documents to an impartial scrutiny that we owe the reconstruction of the historic life of Christ. Underlying such works as the two latest lives of Christ, by Weiss and Beyschlag, there is a mass of painstaking, minute, accurate scholarship, which scans every word of the record with the utmost care.[1] It is this work which is teaching us to know Jesus, not as the stereotype shadow of a man existing in an impossible spectre-world, but as he lived, thought, spoke, and acted. As a picture painted by a great artist differs from the conventional outlines of an heraldic figure, so the life of Christ as we know it now differs from the conventional conception of tradition. We have had to give up many things and some things which perhaps were dear to Christian hearts. Some points are still undecided. But we may rest assured that the main features of the unique picture drawn in our gospels are true. All that we require for our faith is firm. The historic Jesus has stood the test of the most

[1] Compare such works as Weiss's *Matthæus* and *Marcus*.

searching criticism.[1] We need have no fear lest we have built our religion upon an unreality. The scholars who have devoted their energies to an examination of the biblical records claim our gratitude. The battle has been fought; the smoke has not quite cleared away. But to-day the thoughtful Christian stands firmer in his faith because the issue has been faced.[2]

The question of the supernatural forms a separate line of investigation in the historical reconstruction of the life of Christ. It was the fault of the old conception that it found the entire significance of Christ's life in the miraculous. Jesus was nothing more than the conventional figure of a man. The one element in his life in which religious interest centred was the supernatural. It is undeniable that we have passed beyond that view. We are conscious of a decided change in the direction of our religious interest. That change, so far as the life of Jesus is concerned, is the appreciation we have learned to give to his character. We now see in his life, not a tale of magic powers, but rather the ex-

---

[1] The Dutch school, which has gone so far as to deny the existence of Jesus as an historic character, has failed to establish a claim to attention on the part of serious and sober criticism.

Prof. Harnack, in the often-quoted passages of his *Chronologie*, makes outspoken acknowledgment of the retrograde tendency of criticism.

[2] Theological bitterness and that weakness of faith which would put a stop to investigation have unfortunately not yet received the stigma of sin, which in the sight of God must attach to them.

hibition of a human sublimity which makes him unique among men, of that beauty which wrung from the unbeliever Renan the eloquent tribute at the close of his *Life of Jesus*.[1] Our perspective is altered. The human and spiritual claim equal rights with the divine and supernatural.

On the other hand, there are those who are so much impressed with the moral grandeur of Christ's life, that they have pushed the miraculous aside as unessential. At the one end of the scale we have the materialisation of religion, where the ethical is nothing, the miracle everything, and religion becomes superstition. At the other end is the extreme spiritualisation of Christianity. Here the tendency is to abstract religion from physical conditions. Exclusive devotion to the spiritual makes us overlook the sternness of the physical law, and the consciousness of the supernatural in Christianity becomes eliminated. In weak minds this tendency runs into a vague sentimentalism, a feeling with no particular contents; such people simply " feel religious." In strong minds it often goes with a pronounced faith in a present God, a sustaining trust in Providence.

But this sort of spiritualised faith is dangerous. Its fault is that it fails to realise the nature and object of Christianity, and therefore deceives itself with

[1] " Mais quels que puissent être les phénomènes inattendus de l'avenir, Jésus ne sera pas surpassé. Son culte se rajeunira sans cesse : sa légende provoquera des larmes sans fin ; ses souffrances attendriront les meilleurs coeurs ; tous les siècles proclameront qu'entre les fils des hommes, il n'en est pas né de plus grand que Jésus." Closing sentence.

the pretension of being above the physical. We are, as human beings, subject to physical limitations, and it is on account of these very limitations that we need a God. If it were not that I feel the stress of that contradiction in my own being: the spirit with its aspirations for the highest freedom walled up and hemmed in by this " baffling and perverting carnal mesh,"—if it were not for that contradiction between the spiritual and the physical in me, I should not want a God. Therefore, to ignore the physical is absurd. If I am ever to know again that being whose body I have seen lowered into the earth, now no more than a mass of dead matter like the stones and the earth around it, then there must be somewhere a very different world from this. There must be laws of which we can form no conception; there is a secret now closely veiled, when it is revealed a new light will come over the world. We may suppress, but we cannot eradicate, the craving for the supernatural. Why are men so afraid of that word? Science may have its own technical reasons for avoiding it; but for us it seems to express, just as it always did, that something which is beyond our ken, above the natural. The attempts to explain the supernatural in terms of the natural seem very like child's-play. It goes without saying that the supernatural is not contrary to the laws of God; but it is equally evident that no natural law has been discovered which will explain the rising from the dead. We think, sometimes, that we have explained a thing when we have shown that it is not something else;

but we may only have corrected an error or put into accurate language something that everybody knew before. So it is in this case. The human mind has accomplished much, so much, that at times we think we can achieve the impossible; but it is nevertheless a fact, that the mystery of life is no nearer an explanation than it was in the days of Abraham.

It is this mystery of life which we long to pierce. Is there any other than this material universe that we know? Is there nowhere a point of transition from the spiritual to the natural? Has the God to whom we look up nowhere proved his power over the physical? This is the intellectual element in that aspiration which is innate in human nature. We find that Christianity offers an answer to these questions. This answer is in the miraculous element of our gospels.

Doubtless, we must be careful to give no more than its due weight to the miraculous. Let us, therefore, consider the supernatural elements of the gospels. Christ's life is full of the supernatural. It may be questioned whether some of the miracles of Jesus do not receive an adequate and more satisfactory explanation on a natural hypothesis. The question of motive must be given its weight. This applies to such stories as that of the turning of water into wine, and the feeding of the multitude. It is no derogation to the gospel narrative to allow single cases like these to remain open questions. Furthermore, the minute examination and comparison of the synoptic gospels reveals an enlarging tendency in the later in comparison with the earlier version. The story in several cases is amplified by the later writer. This is true of the baptism of Jesus, where the vision of the dove in the original account is made into an actual physical occurrence in St. Luke. Nevertheless, making all allowances for a tendency to amplification and to supernatural explanation, it is impossible to eradicate the miraculous from the story of Jesus. Take as an instance the account of the healing of the paralytic (St. Mark, ii.). Either to explain away the miracle, or to hold that the story is a pure invention, or to disentangle the miraculous and reject it as a later addition: any of these theories presents most serious psychological obstacles. And if the attempt is extended to all the miraculous accounts in the gospels, these difficulties become insuperable. The miracles remain as an integral part of the gospel narrative.

I am by no means attempting to prove the miracles. That is impossible, and the faith that rests upon the miraculous in the story of Christ will prove a failure. All we can show is that the evidence in favour of the miraculous is reasonable, and that it is difficult to explain away. The reasons which induce us to accept that evidence as sufficient are religious, not historical. This applies to the crown of all miracles: the resurrection. The historic evidence for the resurrection of Christ is of the strongest. True, it is not convincing, for many have refused to accept it. But it is quite sufficient for the historic basis of supernatural religion, that the story of the resurrection of Christ is supported by evidence which the candid student must recognise as strong, that it is difficult to account for the narrative upon any theory other than the truth of the fact.

The case is somewhat different with that other article of our creed: the Virgin-birth. The reverential student is reluctant to turn the eye of criticism upon this article of the faith; but it has become an object of dispute, and it would be cowardice, for which we could not answer to God, to turn away from any serious question. First, then, it must be frankly acknowledged that the virgin-birth stands upon no such historic basis as the resurrection. It is not necessary to enter into details. The candid student must concede that, compared with the strength of the evidence for the rising of Christ from the dead, that for the virgin-birth is limited. The fact that this belief was current in the very earliest time, when those were living who might have contradicted it, and that it remained uncontradicted, would be accepted as good evidence of an ordinary occurrence. The magnitude of the fact to be proved and a comparison with the testimony to the truth of the other great miracle make us wish for stronger evidence.

On the other hand, even those who are most keenly aware of the historical difficulty would be reluctant to part with this dogma. The Church through all these ages has accepted it. It would leave us with a sense of incompleteness, of inadequacy, if we had to give up our belief that the entrance of Christianity into the world was without some signal manifestation of God's power. This is more true to-day than it ever was, because we understand the transcendent significance of Christianity to the world as it was never understood before, while at the same time Christianity is seen more and more to be centred in Christ. We are, therefore, intellectually predisposed to accept an account of the beginning of Christianity which should break through the ordinary chain of events.

While, therefore, we consider that we have sufficient grounds for accepting this article of faith, we may not conceal from ourselves that the belief in the virgin-birth rests upon a different basis from the faith in the resurrection. The latter stands upon its own strong evidence. We speak of "the gospel of the resurrection," because it is the story of a risen Christ which through all the ages has touched men's hearts. The article of the virgin-birth on the other hand is in the nature of a corollary to the faith. We reason back to it from the accepted facts of Christ's life. It is a conclusion of which the major premise is the significance of the historic Christ, the minor premise the story in the first chapters of St. Luke. We, therefore, accept the definition which the Church has in all ages acknowledged. But not even the most uncompromising champion of "the faith once delivered to the saints," in its literal interpretation, can fail to appreciate the difference between the assent which we give to the article "conceived by the Holy Ghost, born of the Virgin Mary," and the triumphant conviction with which we profess: "The third day he rose again from the dead."

The question of the miraculous element in the gospels has been obscured because the belief in miracle has been held to be the substance of the faith. Christian faith was made synonymous with the belief in the supernatural. Christ made faith to mean either trust in God or belief in himself, and when he said "believe in me," "come to me," he did not primarily imply belief in the supernatural facts of his life; and when he did include those facts, as in the last chapters of St. John, he included them only as an element of the faith, which was to be far more than an intellectual belief in his divinity. The substance of the Christian faith is the acceptation of Christ as the revelation of God. It is only secondarily, when we reflect upon the faith, that the supernatural enters into it as an element.

The supernatural is not, then, the faith itself; but it undoubtedly is an element in our faith. In the trust which we bestow upon Christ and upon the God whom he revealed, there is always present an undercurrent of feeling which acknowledges his power over the physical world, because Christ exerted that power on earth. The story of the resurrection makes it easier for us to believe. So it has always been. It was by a true instinct that the apostles felt that first and foremost they must be "witnesses of the resurrection." St. Paul gives expression to a genuine Christian experience, when he says: "If in this life only we have hope in Christ, we are of all men most miserable" (1 Cor. xv. 19). Therefore, the spirtual trust in Christ and the belief in the supernatural have always gone together and always will go together in inseparable union. In the normal, healthy Christian faith there is an element of the supernatural.[1]

I have spoken, in another connection, of stages in the growth of faith. We found that the Christian's faith develops, and in the finished flower is something far different from that which it was in the bud. So it is with our belief in Christ. As we are first brought under the influence of his life, our attitude is that of the wanderer who has gone astray and has found a guide; he gives himself up to his guidance without asking many questions. The first faith in Christ is an unquestioning confidence. He who has felt the sweetness and the majesty in the life of Jesus gives up his heart to him; he admits a new spiritual influence into his life. He does not begin by asking himself, Who was Jesus? but by yielding himself to the influence of Jesus. There is in this initial stage no conscious assent to any doctrine of Christ. But gradually the urgency of enquiring thought makes itself felt. The intellectual is closely interwoven

---

[1] "This conclusion (the supernatural power of Christ) belongs in itself to the sphere of religious faith; but rarely has there been a strong faith which has not drawn it." Harnack, *Dogmengeschichte*, vol. i., p. 64, note (third edition).

with the spiritual. We cannot in the long run trust where we do not in some measure understand. The more we feel the moral significance of Christ, the more urgent becomes the necessity of assigning to him his place in the universe. Who, we are driven to ask, was that person who has exerted this influence upon the heart of man and the destinies of the race ? *Was he more than man ?*

This question receives its answer as we learn to understand more fully the inner life of Jesus. The " life of Christ " has become a separate discipline in theological study, and wonderful progress has been made towards a real understanding of that life commensurate with what we demand in the biography of any great character. A mere catalogue of events in their probable sequence, with an inventory of the words of Christ, is not sufficient. Even the illumination of the text from geographical, historical and archæological sources does not touch the real interest of the life of Jesus. We seek to know the inner connection of events. We try to understand the dramatic development of the life, from the enthusiastic beginning, through the growing opposition, to the climax at the feeding of the masses; the increasing devotion to the disciples as the hostility of the people increased ; and then the hurrying forward to the catastrophe. We understand the words of Christ no longer as oracles against a background of eternity, but as discourses spoken to living men, upon questions which were burning issues to Christ himself. The Sermon on the Mount is not a Christian Magna Charta for all times, uttered by Christ for the vast congregation of all generations supposed to have been in his mind at the time; its significance to us lies in the fact that it is the document in which is recorded the answer Jesus made to the most urgent question which confronted him in the course of his ministry—the question of his attitude towards the law. This is one illustration of that deeper insight which it is to-day sought to gain into the life of Jesus. We try to understand Jesus in his relations to the Pharisees, to his disciples, to the people; so also, his position in regard to the national aspirations; and finally, we endeavour to trace his own inner development, the life of the soul in its inner workings. All these elements are a part of that vivid sense of real development in the life of Christ which makes his story so much more human on the one hand, but which at the same time is giving us an increasing appreciation of that which is more than human. For this is what that deeper study of the life of Jesus leads us to. It is one thing to render an homage to a being whom we conceive to have lived a sort of spectral life somewhere midway between humanity and divinity: that homage is not much different from the worship given to idols. It is a very different thing to render the heart's adoration to one whom we have learned to appreciate as the perfection of humanity, but whom for that very reason we are forced to acknowledge as more than man.

I may here emphasise two principles as essential requisites for the better understanding of the life of Jesus. First, the radical point of difference between our estimate of the life of Christ to-day and that which it is superseding is this: Christ was wont to be regarded only for what he achieved *for man;* we are learning to understand Christ primarily for what he achieved for himself, and from the value of his life for himself is deduced his value for others. Our point of view is changed. Consider that remarkable and seemingly incomprehensible utterance spoken by Christ to the man who addressed him, " Good Master, what good thing shall I do that I may have eternal life?" Jesus answered: " Why callest thou me good? there is none good but one, that is, God." (St. Matt. xix. 17.) We cannot understand these words otherwise than as spoken from the consciousness of the task which was committed to him, which he must finish before he could claim the final approval of God. It was his mission, his work, of which Christ spoke elsewhere: " My meat is to do the will of him that sent me, and to finish his work" (St. John, iv. 34), and when he had accomplished it: " I have finished the work which thou gavest me to do" (St. John, xvii. 4). Christ had his life-work as other men have theirs. We have come to speak much of Christ's " mission " or his " vocation," and rightly. For such expressions carry with them this meaning, that Christ, in receiving the Messiahship, assumed a responsibility for his own personal life. It was not that he was all the time looking away from himself to others, but that the solution of his own problem, the consistent carrying out of the will of God in his own life, the maintaining of himself in the position of the " Son of God," was Christ's nearest object. And only so far as he was faithful to the task committed to him, only so far as he carried to a successful issue the commission to which he was divinely ordained, only so far as the problem of his own life was solved, could the benefits of his work flow into the lives of others. The self-determination of Jesus' life according to its own value: this is the point of view from which we are learning to understand him. If Jesus is the world's high-priest, his priesthood has its primary significance for himself. He was high-priest for himself in that he lived his life of communion with God, and only through the satisfaction of the demands of his own personal life could he lead others into that same communion.

The second point is the correction of an error to which is due a certain dualistic conception of Christ's life. This is the dissociation of Christ's death from his life. Theological subtlety has been busy in drawing distinctions. The logical exigency of the plan of salvation, conceived according to the analogy of legal procedure, seemed to require the disintegration of Christ's work into separate elements. While we have quite generally dropped some of these distinctions,—as the distinction between the passive submission of Christ to satisfy the punitive demands of the law, and his active obedience as the foundation

of his vicarious merit in our behalf—the separation
is still made between his active life and the efficacy
of his sacrifice upon the cross. The language of St.
Paul no doubt gives colour to this distinction; we
recall such phrases as: " reconciled to God by the
death of his Son," and the frequent references to
the " cross of Christ ";—it is also true that the belief
in the efficacy of Christ's death is enshrined in our
liturgy and hymns. But if this efficacy is to be
understood in the sense, which is popularly accepted, of a *separate* efficacy, apart from the life, as
the efficacy of a material sacrifice isolated from the
moral acts of his life, to be interpreted according to
the principles of the Hebrew ritual; if the mere extinction of life upon the cross, in close analogy with
the slaughter of animals at the sacrifice in the temple, is the sacrifice to which we look as the foundation of our Christian hope; if to this one act is to be
attributed the overwhelming significance that is
popularly given to it: we are impelled to ask, Why,
then, did not Christ give distinct expression to a
view of himself which on this theory is of such
transcendent importance ? It is not denied that
this view may be extracted from certain sayings of
Christ, such as: " I, when I am lifted up, will draw
all men unto me," "The Son of man came not to
be ministered unto, but to minister, and to give his
life a ransom for many," and " This is my blood of
the new testament, which is shed for many." But
this interpretation is not the natural explanation of
the words of Christ, it is rather read into them from

a preconceived theological opinion whose origin is to be sought elsewhere.

Furthermore, we are led to ask ourselves another question: Wherein consists the efficacy of Christ's act? Here we come to a parting of the ways. We must mark distinctly the divergence of the two answers that may be given, a divergence which is too often blurred over, to the great detriment of clear theological thought. I refer to the distinction already hinted at, between the sacrifice as a mere physical act, the killing of the victim, and the sacrifice as an act of moral submission to the will of God. The first has its origin in materialistic conceptions of the Deity, who is supposed to be gratified by the blood flowing from the victim on the altar. According to this theory, the willingness or unwillingness of the victim is a matter of indifference. The value of the sacrifice depends upon the value of the victim; a costly animal is a more efficacious sacrifice than a poor one, a perfect than an imperfect one. In the case of Christ's sacrifice it was the divinity that gave to the act its value. This value was purely material; it was simply the stamp of a greater efficacy; as a gold coin is worth more than silver, so the God-victim is worth more than a man-victim would be. The conception of the death of Christ under this theory moves altogether within physical and materialistic limits. But, we are forced to ask, what sort of a God is it who delights in the mere extinction of life, the agonies of the death-struggle, the flowing of the blood? It is impossible, when the true bearings of this theory are held before the mind and when it is traced in its antecedents and to its consequences, not to see how incompatible the idea of a material sacrifice is with the Christian doctrine of a spiritual God. Few, therefore, will be found who hold this doctrine in its purity. There is generally an underlying consciousness that the value of Christ's sacrifice was determined by his submission. According to the idea which St. Paul expresses, he "humbled himself and became *obedient* unto death." Here the moral quality in the act comes into play. But we frequently fail to realise that with this admission an altogether new and different face is put upon the act of Christ. This theory is exclusive of the other. It is no longer the physical act of Jesus which is pleasing to God, which formed the "sacrifice" to which we refer the salvation of man.

How, then, can the sacrificial value of Christ's obedience be confined to his death? Where did that value begin? On the cross? or with the crown of thorns? in the garden of Gethsemane? Where, in other words, shall we draw the line at which Christ's moral submission begins to have the value of sacrifice which before it had not? Christ certainly suffered before the cross and before Gethsemane; and the suffering which he underwent throughout the course of his ministry came to him through the same cause as that upon the cross: namely, his obedience to the divine will. It is clear that we shall involve ourselves in inextricable difficulties, if, having accepted the moral value of Christ's sufferings, we endeavour to maintain the distinction between the sufferings of his death and those of his life. It is true that the sufferings and the obedience reached their climax on the cross; and this very simple consideration will explain those references in St. Paul's writings in which he seems to ascribe exclusive virtue to the death upon the cross, as well as the liturgical expressions to the same effect. We still speak of the cross of Christ as the great act of sacrifice, and rightly. But it need not be implied in that phrase that the death and its suffering had an efficacy apart from the life; we mean rather that in the death upon the cross there is brought to the culminating point, and we see in it an emblem of, that principle which Christ embodied perfectly in his human life, by which he became the Saviour of the world: obedience to the will of God.

"My meat is to do the will of him that sent me and to finish his work": those words are the full expression of Christ's mission. His life is summed up in the one word—obedience. What would have been had the Jews accepted him, we cannot even guess. As it was, that obedience demanded his submission to the most cruel death at the hands of those to whose service he had given himself. So understood, Christ's life becomes unified under one great principle, and we are freed from the barren sophistical distinctions in which theology had become involved.

I have said that a growing faith is at a certain

point brought before the question: Was Christ more than man? The way to answer that question, we found, was by a sympathetic study of the historic life of Christ, for which I have pointed out certain guiding principles. Now we come to formulate the answer.

The first step in this process is the recognition of Christ as the revelation of God. There is this peculiarity about his life that it is always pointing away from itself to God. Christ makes God known to us. In his inner life we read the heart of the Father. We recognise the significance of the statement: " God .... hath in these last days spoken unto us by his son " (Heb. i. 2).

This leads us to the next step of the enquiry. Christ being the revelation of God implies a certain participation in divinity. How then shall we define his personality?

The question of the person of Christ was the burning problem of the early Christian ages and was disputed in the ecumenical councils. The definitions set forth by these councils do not help us much. That of the two natures is simply a logical definition. For the time when they were made such definitions were doubtless sufficient; historically, they are very important. They do not satisfy us, because to say that two things go together, when we cannot form any conception of the process, conveys little meaning to us. You cannot deceive yourself into believing that you have accomplished much by putting the two natures together and calling them one person, when you cannot define a human nature, and have no conception what a divine nature is. There is indeed great danger from the misinterpretation of this article. It is the danger which the treatment of spiritual subjects always carries with it: that we should forget that after all we conceive of spiritual things only by concrete analogies, and that we imagine the two natures existing side by side as material objects do.

The important truth conveyed by the definition of Christ's person in Article II. is, that he was both perfect Man and perfect God. But just here the real problem begins. How shall we explain and realise the co-existence of the two ? The docetic doctrine, which made Christ's humanity a mere pretence, is supposed to have been ruled out by the Chalcedonian formula; yet the popular conceptions of our day are a close approach to docetism. Christ is asserted to have been man, but there is an implied understanding that he was not confined by the limitations of humanity. He was omniscient and omnipotent, even if he did not use his powers, or but rarely. But where, we may ask, if these divine attributes are granted, does there remain any mark of his humanity except the human body ? We can hardly escape the conclusion that upon this theory the humanity of Christ was something worse than a fiction: a deception. The " communicatio idiomatum," invented to explain the mystery, is useless: a mere trick of words without any reality. The candid student finds himself forced to make one concession after another: Christ was not gifted with omniscience where the interests of his work were not involved; Christ did not necessarily have at his disposal all human knowledge in all its branches; he did not possess omnipotent power for every conceivable purpose. But these concessions make it evident that we can form no conception of Christ with his divinity and his humanity both equally active.

A way out of the difficulty was supposed to have been found in the doctrine of the Kenosis. The divinity was in abeyance during the earthly life of the Saviour. This doctrine is largely held to-day. As a confession of ignorance concerning the metaphysical Godhead of Christ, it may be accepted. As a full explanation of the Christological problem, it is quite inadequate. It shares with the other view, which it superseded, this vitiating fault: it regards the problem solely on its metaphysical side. It sets itself to answer this question: granted a God entering the human sphere, wherein can we trace the divinity? And the answer given is correct, *so far as it goes:* it denies the possibility of a metaphysical knowledge of the Godhead. But the doctrine of the Kenosis, by asserting that the divinity is hidden, in abeyance, remains a prisoner in the fatal meshes of metaphysical reasoning. That conception of Christ which simply asserts his metaphysical Godhead as an article of cold, intellectual belief, which fails to trace the meaning of that Godhead in the earthly life and to appreciate the significance of it as a fact of Christ's life *for me*, for my religious interests, which does not make the divinity of Christ a present fact of my own experience: this conception falls by many degrees below the Christian level; it moves within a sphere of thought which is proper, not to Christian worship, but to heathen idolatry.

We again ask: granted a God entering human life, wherein can we trace the divinity? And the answer is this: the marks of the divinity must be found in the moral and the spiritual sphere. Renouncing all attempt to exceed the powers of the human mind, we may affirm that Christ, in his life upon earth, perfectly revealed the being of God, *so far as it is possible to reveal God in human form*. This statement is based upon the recognition of two facts: first, that there is a sphere of truth which belongs to the infinite, which is beyond the world of phenomena. The latter alone is known to us. We are not gifted with faculties to penetrate into the eternal reality behind. So far as we can conceive any being from the world of eternal reality entering into man's life, it can only be—for our knowledge—under laws known to us. But, secondly, there is one sphere in which man stands even now above time, in eternity: that is, the moral and spiritual. It is given to us to have some knowledge of the divine in the sphere of God's moral and spiritual laws. Therefore, if we would know the God in Christ, we must know him in his moral and spiritual relations.

Just here, the study of the gospels has opened a mine of infinite wealth. We can do no more than glance at a few particulars, to see how the deeper study of Christ's life has strengthened the belief in him as the unique among men, as the perfect revelation of God in human life. Let us take the story of the Christ-child in the temple. It throws the only ray of light upon the maturing consciousness of Jesus. He had been fascinated by the novel interests of the temple and new thoughts seemed to take hold of him. His answer to his mother revealed that a turning-point had been reached in his development: " Wist ye not that I must be about *my* father's business ?" Here is a child of twelve years who uses an expression which no human being, before or since, has dared to use. God had been a father to Israel, Christ taught his followers to pray: " *Our* Father who art in heaven ;" but no individual has ever been aware of such a relationship to God that he could look up and call him: " *my* father." We can explain the expression on the lips of the child in no other way than upon the assumption that there came at this time into his mind the feeling of a relation to God, closer, more intimate, than that between God and any other human being. And by this light we can understand in some degree the growth of the child. The knowledge of himself came to him slowly, with the developing consciousness; and it came to him, not as a knowledge of superhuman endowment, nor as an insight into the metaphysical relation between him and God, but through the growing sense of being in a special way the object of the divine love.

In the mature life of Christ we can trace his divinity, not so much by the miracles, as in the moral and spiritual grandeur with which he is invested. Sometimes, it shows itself in a startling utterance, and then we are afforded one of those precious glimpses into the workings of his consciousness. So, when he boldly challenges his opponents: "Which of you convinceth me of sin?" No cloud of moral imperfection could dim the consciousness of one, who, as sober and far removed from fanaticism as Christ was, could make this unheard-of claim. But it is more especially in his action, in the tenor of his life, that we trace the God in Christ: in the harmonious mingling of womanly tenderness with manly courage, in that majesty which forced even from the rude soldiers their involuntary tribute in the garden of Gethsemane, in the compassion for all pain and weakness, in the meekness of the sufferer. Above all, we trace it in one marvellous manifestation. I have already spoken of it. It is his mastership. We recognise it in the impression we get from his life, that whatever his situation, Christ was always superior to it. It is the unbroken calmness of his life, testifying to an unconquerable self-confidence. Contrast Christ's attitude towards God and his attitude to men. Towards God, a constant expectation, a waiting upon the divine guidance, a hearkening for the voice by which to shape his course: an attitude of utter and complete dependence. On the other hand, in his relations towards men, with his intense sympathy for all things human and his readiness to accept men's sympathy: a complete absence of dependence. Where we anxiously watch the effect of our actions, where success or failure so largely determines our conduct, where we alternate between hopes and fears, enthusiasm and despondency, we see in Christ a serene elevation above the vicissitudes of his career, a persistent maintenance of faith in his cause undisturbed by opposition and apparent failure, a persevering belief in human nature, an unconquerable hope for the future and a steadfastness of purpose which is neither the doggedness of obstinacy nor the blindness of enthusiasm. It is this which is the wonder of Christ's life.

No painter has yet caught the spell of such a scene as that of Christ before Pilate. When Christian art, which in a Sistine Madonna came so near the ideal of the womanly, shall succeed in setting before us the true Christ in that scene; then, in the manly grasp of life, in the superiority to his situation, which his features will display, it will teach us to realise better than before the divinity of the Son of Man. It is beyond our faculties to comprehend how the infinite could be incarnate in the human; but it is not beyond our faculties to trace in the spiritual and moral life of Christ the marks of divine character.

We must not fail to distinguish, as has here been done, between the practical and metaphysical divinity of Christ. In what I have just now said I have been treating of the practical divinity. It is that belief in Christ which enters directly as a motive into our life. Christ is the perfect revelation of God, and therefore is God to me. In his life, and in it alone, I learn to know God. In Christ it has pleased God to make himself known to man. It is "God manifest in the flesh," so far as God can be manifest, when the eternal enters into the sphere of the finite. This is the saving truth upon which the soul feeds.

The human mind obeys an irresistible impulse in enquiring into the metaphysical foundation. It asks: what is the essential relation of Christ to the Father? What was the mode of his being before he appeared in the flesh? Here is the rightful sphere of dogma. It goes beyond the historical conditions to the metaphysical foundation; it presents the conditions of the practical; it pursues the antecedents to the last conclusion.

The confounding of the practical and the metaphysical has been the fruitful source of misunderstanding. Dogma represents the metaphysical foundation. It is necessary. Athanasius fought the battle for the metaphysical divinity of Christ, and the Church has held fast to his assertion of it. But if the practical belief in Christ's revelation is insufficient without the doctrine, it is equally true that the doctrine without the vital conviction is useless.[1] Nothing is more shallow than a mere as-

[1] Doctrine is the skeleton under the flesh and blood. The late bishop of Massachusetts was persecuted and his memory is still being persecuted, because, for gross eyes, he did not make the skeleton sufficiently protrude from under the body of flesh and blood, as he with his inimitable skill painted it.

sertion of the divinity of Christ without any knowledge of its meaning. It is the form of religion without its power, and the form often covers the grossest practical infidelity.

We may not forget that metaphysics is not religion. When St. Thomas exclaimed to the risen Christ: " My Lord and my God," his words expressed a religious conviction. The statement of the creed " God of God, Light of Light, very God of very God " is the speculative conclusion from the religious fact. It is not religion but theology.

CHAPTER VII.

THE ETHICAL DETERMINATION OF THE CHRISTIAN LIFE.

THE kingdom of God comprehends two distinct elements of human life, its religious and its ethical determination. The religious is a separable element; the primary factor in Christian character is the normal relation to God in Christ. We now proceed to consider the ethical basis of the kingdom of God. I shall attempt no systematic treatment, but shall endeavour to indicate the lines which must be followed in order to obtain a full appreciation of the term " kingdom of God " as used by Christ.

We may complete the formal definition. The kingdom of God is the sphere in which man approaches God. But it is something more; another condition enters into it. That condition is the ethical regulation of life, the organisation of human society in accordance with the will of God. It embraces the fulfilment of duty to self and to others. The ideal of the one side of the Christian life is to *be* right, the ideal of the other is to *do* right. In the one it is a question of the state in which a man is, in the other it is a question of man's conduct. The contrast is the familiar one of faith and works. Faith is the essential principle of the Christian life. But when you have established yourself in Christian faith, the question still is, What am I *to do* as a Christian? Christ gave abundant attention to this side of the Christian life. He recognised the ancient law and commanded us to love God and to love our neighbour. He bade men be merciful, not to judge, be perfect, not to swear, not to retaliate, not to take unnecessary thought, to be wise, to be liberal, to honour parents, to deny themselves, to be watchful, to be faithful; he taught the sacredness of marriage and of the family; he held up to scorn the hypocrisy of the Pharisees; he taught a nicer discrimination of moral value. In all this and much more, Jesus points out the ethical basis of his kingdom. We may, therefore, define the kingdom of God to be that new society inaugurated by Jesus, whose fundamental principles consist, first, in the re-establishment of man's normal relation to God, secondly, in the organisation of human relationships according to the laws of God.

Is that dualism definitive? This is the question that has puzzled the Christian mind ever since St. Paul wrote that man is saved by faith, and St. James that man is saved by works. The human mind craves above all things unity. The case now before us presents a peculiarly difficult problem, and the great intellectual effort spent upon it has not discovered a satisfactory solution. We see an illustration of this effort at unification in our article " Of Good Works " (No. XII), where it is asserted that they " do spring out necessarily of a true and lively faith; insomuch that by them a lively Faith may be as evidently known as a tree discerned by the fruit." As far as this sentence is true it presents a barren tautology. For faith is simply made to include the motive to good works; and then, of course, the good works "necessarily" follow upon faith. But this inclusive definition of faith is not one that can be universally applied. So, too, the decree on justification of the Council of Trent presents an elaborate attempt at reconciling faith and works; with the result, however, of an aimless vacillation between the two poles of Christian experience.

We may say, as Ritschl does, that the Christian life is not like the circle, but like the ellipse, revolving around two points; but that does not explain it. This is a physical analogy and another illustration of the incompleteness of this sort of reasoning. The stars which revolve in ellipses obey the laws of nature. The human will differs from the star in that it has the choice of disobedience, and we want to find the answer to this very question, Why should I obey the laws of the ellipse rather than the simple law of the one centre? In like manner, when we say that good works are both the signs and the organs of faith, we express an important truth, namely, that by good works we recognise the man's disposition, and that the disposition is strengthened by the practice of good works. We may also say that each is practically necessary to the other. You cannot do life's work without peace with God, and you cannot live near God without doing your duty. But with all these explanations we have not established unity of principle. We cannot imagine a finished Christian character without either faith or good works. But why does not the right relationship to God include the right relationship to man? Why can we not sum up the whole Christian life in one comprehensive principle? That we cannot do this seems to be the plain teaching of experience. Whatever our faith is, however strong, however perfect our trust in God, duty always faces us in the shape of a resolution; we have to make up our minds to do what is right; and when, as often is the case, this making up our minds involves the overcoming of a certain amount of repugnance in the shape of the love of ease or shrinking from effort, so far from the action flowing naturally out of the motive, as the sound does upon the blow of the hammer, it requires the bringing up of the forces of our moral nature, with the implied expenditure of more or less moral energy.

Mr. Spencer maintains that the sense of duty or moral obligation is transitory; with the advance of civilisation a time will come when it will be entirely cast off, when man will have become so used to doing the right thing that it will be impossible for him to do anything else. If the dream is ever realised in the way Mr. Spencer imagines, then man will have ceased to be man and will have become a machine. The Christian also looks forward to the state in which the sense of duty shall cease to be a coercive power, but it will be under different conditions and in another world. In this earthly sphere it is hardly worth while to trouble ourselves much with these speculations. If there should ever be a prospect that a man should leave his bed on a cold winter's night in response to a call of duty without the necessity of a moral effort to overcome the physical repugnance, then we shall be ready to give serious attention to Mr. Spencer's prophecy. In the meantime we shall have to deal with duty as something which is often very disagreeable, and which requires strong motives to make us do it. In fact, we have a suspicion, as already stated, that we shall have to be more careful about our motives in the future than we ever were before.

We are forced to the conclusion, that the dualism of the religious and the ethical determination of the Christian life is insurmountable. Practically there is no way out. We shall never get beyond the effort. It is only the fanaticism of a pagan mysticism that can ever say: I have arrived at that perfection of the Christian life, I have so united myself to God, than sin is not for me. When a man gives up watching himself, when he yields to the delusion that no more effort is required of him, when his life ceases to be a moral struggle, he has entered upon the downward path.

But if the dualism cannot be reduced, it can be explained. The explanation is in the fact of sin. Sin is a radical disturbance in our relations, a lack of harmony in our nature. "The spirit is willing, but the flesh is weak." The dualism of principle in the religious life is owing to the disharmony of our nature. But normal humanity is not a sinful humanity. We can conceive of a life without the disturbing element of sin. Such would be the normal life. In this normal life there would be but one principle, that of man's complete union with God. With the disturbance of that normal relation through sin came in the other principle, the ethical, the necessity of law, of effort. Without sin, the performance of duty would be natural; or rather, there would be no duty, no law. Life would be all towards God, summed up in one principle: fellowship with God. To that state we believe we shall come, but in another world. In this life we must be satisfied to get on as well as we can under a necessary dualism. It will always carry with it uncertainty and vacillation. At this moment you will feel yourself in a state of peaceful fellowship with God; it is the joy of your life. But presently that peace is disturbed by the insistent question, Have I done all my duty? To harmonise the two is the Christian's great difficulty. To find the right mean between the satisfaction of stern duty and the enjoyment of the sense of security in God is one of the perplexities of life. We can never expect to arrive at a state of perfect harmony in this life, because there will always be that jarring between the ethical and the religious.

We can now see the element of truth in the contention which Mr. Spencer makes. The ethical *is* transitory; but it will pass away only under other conditions of life; then it will be engulfed in the complete union and fellowship with God. There will be a time when goodness, justice, virtue, and all other terms denoting ethical value, will have no meaning, because their present significance is derived only from their opposite, which is sin. In that world where the spiritual will be in complete mastery, sin will be no more. We can see also how there is even here an approach to that state. With the repeated performance of duty, duty becomes easier. The ethical law tends to be minimised, as man grows into closer religious fellowship with God. That it will ever disappear in this life, and that with it duty and sin will be eliminated from the vocabulary of human nature, is a phantom of the scientific brain.

It is a far-reaching principle of human life that the higher law tends to supplant the lower. Man is relieved from subjection to law, but only on condition that he yields himself to the higher law. In savage life the ruling principle is very much the same as in the brute-world: ceaseless rivalry and competition. The result is, only the fittest survive. As man advances in civilisation he learns to substitute another principle, that of co-operation; the sense of human solidarity, the feeling of human sympathy, has largely overcome the old order of things in which every man was for himself. The consequence is, that the law of the survival of the fittest is to a considerable extent superseded. Men and women survive, who for some shortcoming, physical or moral, would not have survived under the old system.

The story of this vast complex life of ours is the story of the delicate balance between the two laws, the lower and the higher.'

Our penal methods illustrate how the higher relieves the lower law. A man has committed a crime. The law says he must suffer. It cares nothing for the man, only for the retaliation. In a rough way the mere punishment of crime works for the purification of society by cutting the diseased parts out of the body politic. But we have become aware that there is another law, often more effective than the law of retaliation: the law of human sympathy. Men have been touched and reformed by the power of sympathy where the mere force of punishment has proved powerless.

This progress from the lower to the higher explains the relation between the ethical and the religious in the Christian life. The beginning is with the ethical. The law was before Christ. Man must first learn the difference between right and wrong. But as he advances, he comes more and more under the sway of another principle: his relation to God tends to fill his life, and the ethical law grows less

---

[1] This fact of the two laws running through our life is one of the utmost importance, and if kept in view would clear up many misunderstandings. Compare Gordon, *The Christ of To-Day*, p. 88: "Granted that the necessity for the ferocious egoism in animal existence is an absolute mystery, the fact that it is a vanishing force, and that from the first it is clearly under the ascendancy of another force, the altruistic impulse of parenthood, pours a flood of light through the whole wild process of nature." Even in the brute-world there is this foreshadowing of the twofoldness of law governing life.

exacting, because it has become a part of his nature. The end of the process will be in another world, where the ethical will be no more, because it is absorbed in the one permanent, constant principle of human life: union with God. These considerations satisfy the mind which craves for unity, by showing that the present dualism, though necessary for the time, is abnormal, due to man's abnormal condition, and will eventually yield to a permanent unity of principle.

We found, in treating of the religious determination of the Christian life, that Christ sets forth God as the object of his revelation. It was his mission to reveal God and to bring man to the fellowship with God. Man's religious life centres in God. Where, we now ask, does the ethical life centre? What is the Christian's ethical end and purpose? What is his final authority, his moral guide? This question is one of the most important man can ask himself.

Let us examine the records. Christ established the kingdom of God. He must have had in mind what was to be the final authority for the subjects of that kingdom. Christ did not institute the kingdom as something new: it was as the fulfilment of the old, as the bringing to its appointed completion of all that the old covenant contained, as the culmination of the ancient history, that the kingdom of God came into the world. It was no revolution, but the growing of the bud into the flower. Therefore Christ recognised the revelation of the Old Testament and the validity of the Old Testament law. If the interpretation which he gave was more spiritual and free, yet he did not absolve his followers from obedience to the law. Therefore the question of the obligation of the Jewish law in the Christian Church became the first burning question. With the accession of large numbers of Gentiles to the Christian fold there could be but one answer to that question. Those who believe in Providence cannot resist the conclusion that St. Paul was especially raised up, one of those rare characters who by the power of their personal influence change the destinies of mankind, in order that the Church in this supreme crisis might be led into the path of universal religion. To-day, the Church unanimously accepts the verdict of St. Paul which cast off the trammels of Judaism. We still ask ourselves, doubtfully, How do we reconcile this with the very positive statements of Christ, which seem to make the Jewish law binding? But we think we can see how Christ himself was preparing the way for a larger conception of religion. His spiritual view foreshadowed a time when the law would lose its significance. He looked into a future where men should no more worship God either in Jerusalem or on Gerizim; he recognised a spiritual worship of God above the worship of material sacrifices. He spoke of the temple as transitory.

On the other hand, the very kingdom which he announced presupposed a king. Accordingly, we find it implied in some of Jesus' words, that the authority of a living king would be supreme among his followers. To his disciples he says, "I am with you alway, even unto the end of the world." And when he made this promise he could not have thought of his continued presence otherwise than as their Master, their King.

We do well to dwell upon this claim to kingship which Christ made, as showing what in his mind was intended to be the final court of appeal, the last authority, of the Christian. The time was to come when this claim should be forgotten, neglected, put aside, despoiled of its meaning, in favour of a theory which, reverting to the Hebrew conception of a written law, has by the almost unanimous consent of Christendom exercised a controlling authority: the theory of biblical infallibility, which teaches that the last authority for the Christian in the ethical and the spiritual sphere is the written word.

We are thus brought face to face with this theory. It is necessary that we should define our position towards it, because it concerns us at this point to know what is the final ethical authority in the kingdom of God. But aside from that, the discussion of every theological question proceeds upon a certain conception of the Bible, and whoever undertakes such a discussion is bound to state the theory of the Bible upon which he takes his stand. No full treatment can, of course, be entered into here. Results only can be given, with a brief reference to the methods by which these results are reached. I shall deal only with the New Testament. There are interesting and important questions which concern the

Old Testament, but the New Testament is the key to the problem, and it is from New Testament studies that we have gained the most decisive results.

I shall sum up what I have to say about the authority of the New Testament under three heads. First, those methods will be set forth which alone promise satisfactory results. Secondly, the conclusions will be drawn. Thirdly, certain bearings of the traditional theory will be considered.

I. First, as to the proper methods by which the question of biblical authority is to be studied. One cannot help wondering, as volume after volume appears, treating of the Bible, its authority, and inspiration, from an *à priori* point of view, why it seems so rarely to occur to anyone that the only way to answer these questions is by a study of the facts, by finding out what the Bible contains, and its history, and then drawing the conclusions. This is the method of procedure followed in all other branches of investigation: conclusions are drawn from an accurate knowledge of the facts. Not so with the Bible. Inspiration is supposed to be something which can be determined quite aside from the thing which is inspired; consequently a whole library of literature exists upon what the Bible ought to be, little regard being paid to what it is. This remarkable attitude towards the Bible was noticed long ago by Richard Hooker, who, at the end of the third Book of the *Ecclesiastical Polity*, speaks as follows of those who prove their point by arguing that God *must* have taught certain things in the Bible: ". . . they do as if one should demand a legacy by force and virtue of some written testament, wherein there being no such thing specified, he pleadeth that there it must needs be, and bringeth arguments from the love or goodwill which always the testator bore him; imagining, that these or the like proofs will convict a testament to have that in it which other men can nowhere by reading find." And then he lays down this principle which every theologian, and especially every Bible student, would do well to adopt as his own: "In matters which concern the actions of God, the most dutiful way on our part is to search what God hath done, and with meekness to admire that, rather than to dispute what he in congruity of reason ought to do." The last words of this quotation describe what has been done with the Bible; men have disputed "what in congruity of reason God ought to do." Therefore it is that no satisfactory conclusion has been reached. No conclusion ever can be reached by means of the *à priori* method employed. If those who feel the unrest of public opinion upon this question hope ever to put an end to it, and so to satisfy a universal desire for light, it can only be done by breaking forever with the irrational method too often followed and devoting themselves to a thorough investigation into the text of the New Testament and the history of the canon.

For there are these two departments of investigation, with which we are here concerned.¹ (1) The

---

¹ To these might be added a third: the discipline of comparative religion. But this is more uncertain in its conclusions. At any rate,

study of the history of the canon has been most fruitful of results. We are now in a position to understand the several steps by which the New Testament took its present shape and assumed its authority. The one thing which here is significant is the entire absence of any uniform principle in the formation of the canon. A number of tendencies co-operating produced the result. There was the need of writings to supply the place of absent apostles. Then there was the authority inherent in the words of Christ, the λόγοι κυρίου, which from the beginning stood on a level with the Old Testament. Then there was the public reading after the custom of the synagogue, which tended to give a certain sanctity to the writings. There was also the stress of the times, which made the defenders of the faith against heretics look for some authority to which to appeal. The result of these various forces is seen in the gathering together of a certain number of documents to meet the practical necessities of the Churches. The various parts acquired authority in various ways and finally were bound together in one volume and became our New Testament.

Only a willful distortion of historical facts is able to obliterate this lack of unity of principle. Why the study of the text and of the history of the canon are abundantly sufficient for the absolute certainty of the conclusions here set forth. So inveterate is the prejudice upon this subject, that not until the student has worked his way to a satisfactory solution by the road here suggested will in most cases the question present itself in its full clearness: What is the basis of this colossal doctrine of biblical infallibility?

was St. Mark included in the canon ? or St. Luke ? or the Acts ? or St. Jude ? or the Epistle to the Hebrews ? Upon what principle were the writings of Barnabas, Clement and Hermas excluded ? To these questions even Origen in the third century could find no answer but the authority of tradition. And we are to-day obliged to acknowledge tradition as practically the only principle which gives authority to our New Testament. Nor was this principle altogether decisive, as the long disputes about the Antilegomena prove, and such facts as that an Epistle to the Laodiceans was added to the Pauline epistles in England in the ninth century or that the Pastor of Hermas was used as late as the twelfth century.

No doubt the tradition of the Church, the almost universal usage of Christendom for many ages, is an authority to which we owe every respect. No doubt we must reverently recognise the hand of God in preserving these documents of the earliest Christianity through these many ages. But if God had willed that these writings should be the absolutely infallible record of his will, would he not have given us some more convincing proof than appears from our present knowledge of the way they came into being and were incorporated in the canon ?

(2) The most important factor in the decision of the question is the examination of the New Testament itself. Here the gospels chiefly claim our attention. The study of the gospels has been prosecuted with a minuteness and a keenness of analysis which probably has no parallel in the field

of literary criticism, with the result that the human workmanship of these writings is laid bare and we can see how they came into being.

Not only is it well understood that the gospels are interdependent among themselves : the original document underlying the synoptic account has been deciphered with considerable certainty and printed both in the Greek and in English.[1] Variations from this original gospel and of the gospels among themselves, together with many curious phenomena, such as the recurrence of the same words in different contexts, are accounted for.

Very little idea, however, can be given of the force of the argument, because it is cumulative. Its cogency depends not upon a few, but upon hundreds of observations, which altogether make the case so clear that no candid mind can refuse to accept the conclusions.

We are here not dealing with something intangible, a philosophical conception, an abstruse idea; we have to do with a book, which has had an origin and a history. All that is claimed is something of the same conscientiousness and patience in the examination of the words of this book that a Darwin

[1] Prof. Bernhard Weiss, *Das Marcusevangelium*, etc., and Jolley, *The Synoptic Problem*. It is not claimed that the theory represented by these writers is in all parts correct or that the " original gospel," as it is given, is in every word identical with *the* original gospel.

The subject seemed to call for some reference in the text to the methods of study, beyond a bald statement of the results. Of course, I have given the briefest possible indications of these methods, along the line of which I have studied for many years.

gave to the phenomena of life when he was tracing the laws of nature. If Darwin had only reasoned about what God ought to have done, he never would have accomplished what he did, but with far more reverence than many a Bible student shows he sought to find out what God has done.

II. What are the results? Attention has been largely confined to the criticism of the Old Testament. Here many problems remain unsolved and the reconstruction of history, which has been so startling, is not yet fully carried through. In the New Testament, also, there are questions awaiting definite answer. Probably, we shall never have certainty upon many of these. But we must not allow this fact to escape our notice: that the criticism of the New Testament has established one result which is incontestable. This result is one of the most important acquisitions of human knowledge in modern times. It is negative in form, but it is most positive in the results that flow from it. It is the definite destruction of the theory of infallibility.

When we speak of an infallible writing, we mean that that writing has been preserved by divine influence from error, either of any kind, or—as the limitation is now sometimes made—error in the religious sphere; that, therefore, we can use this writing as an oracle, the direct voice of God. Infallibility, in either sense, it is impossible to ascribe to the New Testament.

It cannot be too strongly insisted upon that this is no longer an open question—except to prejudice and ignorance. We consider mathematical truth to be the most certain of all theoretical knowledge. The proof for the conclusion here set forth is in cogency equal to mathematical proof—for those who will study, not the *à priori* possibility or probability of any theory of inspiration, but the contents of our New Testament and the history of the canon.¹

It is a mercy, in which we cannot but discern the guiding hand of God, that the Protestant Episcopal Church is not committed to any statement of infallibility. It is another mercy, for which we are devoutly thankful, that the Church has been led to embody in her constitution the one expression which most fitly, most fully, as no other word does, sums up the meaning of the Bible for the Christian: "The word of God." It expresses precisely what

¹ The lack of precision in the use of terms is a most fruitful source of misunderstanding and confusion in theology. This is especially true of the terms "infallibility" and "authority." They are often used as synonymous, and he who denies the infallibility of the Bible is supposed to deny its authority. And yet in ordinary language the terms are not confused. We speak of the "authority" of parents. But the strictest advocate of parental authority would not claim infallibility for parents. So, we may ascribe to the Bible a very decided and high authority and yet disbelieve in its infallibility. And if we thus discriminate between the terms we find that the question of fallibility or infallibility is the crux of the biblical problem. When we have settled that, the question of the Bible is settled without any further words, and it will be unnecessary to enter into detail in regard to the conclusions to be drawn from a denial of infallibility, such as that we can be absolutely sure of no single word or sentence that it was so uttered by Christ as we have it.

we believe of the Bible. To change the phrase, the Bible is the word of God, into, the Bible contains the word of God, is to change one of the most striking and accurate definitions ever given into a meaningless formula.

In interpreting the expression, we notice first that it is the *word*, not the *words*; this makes a vast difference. Furthermore, we must let the Bible itself interpret the expression. St. Paul uses it. We read in 1 Thess. ii. 13: "For this cause also thank we God without ceasing, because when ye received the word of God which ye heard of us, ye received it not as the word of men, but as it is in truth, the word of God, which effectually worketh also in you that believe." Here the contrast is between the word of men and the word of God. There is not the slightest indication, nor the remotest probability, that St. Paul had in mind any infallibility as belonging to this "word of God." What did he have in mind? One great fact: Salvation in Christ, and any word which would set before men that one fact was the word of God. To him it was the message of man's release from bondage into the liberty of Christ. He did not have to enquire whether every particular statement of that message was true.

Let us take an illustration: A garrison is surrounded and besieged. Many days they have held out; the utmost distress prevails. Suddenly a messenger appears: he has broken through the enemy's lines. He brings news of relief. It means life from death to that garrison. Do we suppose they will ask the messenger many inquisitive questions, and if he cannot tell them the exact number of the relieving army, and where it came from, and the names and appearance of the officers, and the nature of their accoutrements, they will not believe his message? Will they concern themselves about these trifling details when release from sure death is at hand? That was what Christianity was to St. Paul, and the news of that release was the word of God. And when we use St. Paul's expression to designate what we understand the Bible to be, we mean that it is the message of salvation from God to mankind. We cannot think it strange that the message comes to us in imperfect form, for the messengers after all were men and fallible, but we none the less accept their message as "the word of God."

III. So far the results. There remains something to be said about the bearings of these results. One cannot dwell long upon these reflections without being forcibly struck with the greatness of the contrast between St. Paul's use of the expression "word of God" and what the expression came to mean in later ages. The spirit of St. Paul went out of the Church, and the "liberty wherewith Christ hath made us free" was no longer understood and valued. The "word of God" lost its meaning as the message of man's salvation, and it became "the words of God." As such it stood for the sum of all the sentences in the Bible. This carried with it the belief that God had sent to man, not the message of redemption, but an oracle, in which all parts were of equal value as coming direct from the divine author. It was a radical departure from the view of St. Paul, and such a departure as he would have been the first to deplore. For it was a relapse into the spirit of that narrow Judaism against which he fought so persistently. It was the revival of the law; it put law once more into the central place of religion. The very essence of the new religion was that it came as the fulfilment of the promise contained in the old. So Christ understood it, and therefore he was always calling men to believe in him. So St. Paul understood it; to him the gospel meant just one thing: Christ has lived and died to save man, to bring him to God. The new interpretation of the "word of God" made the gospel mean something entirely different. Instead of one simple truth, it was a thousand things that men were required to believe. The character of Christianity was changed. Not Christ, but the Bible, became the mediator between God and man. The answer to the soul craving peace was not the message of one who lived and died for man, but an atomistic law of infinitely diversified aspect. Law and gospel have always been used as terms of mutually exclusive antithesis, and the Christian gospel is held to mark a higher level of religion than the law; therefore the altered conception of Christianity, which is distinguished by the atomistic legal view of the Bible, denotes a distinct retrogression to a lower level of religion.

One feels the obligation to deal very conscientiously with an opinion which has held its ground so persistently and to measure words carefully in judging it. But whoever has made himself acquainted with the facts in question, who realises what the bearings of the traditional theory of Bible authority are, who is in a position to measure the influence of this theory upon religious life and character, can hardly doubt that it represents one of the most serious aberrations of Christianity that is to be met with in the course of its history.

What has been said about the relapse from the gospel to the law may be held to be an exaggeration. It will be maintained that those who hold most strongly to the infallibility of the Scriptures insist no less strenuously upon the redemption by Christ. This is true. But one of these truths must be fundamental. They cannot, and they do not, exist side by side; they are not held independently the one of the other, as two equally important truths. As a matter of fact, the belief in the Bible is the first. Here lies the gravamen of the matter. Belief in the Bible is fundamental; belief in Christ depends upon belief in the Bible—not in the sense in which this is necessarily true of every belief in Christ, namely, that it rests upon credence given to the New Testament as historical documents, just as we believe any other facts upon the evidence given. Belief in Christ, according to this view, depends upon belief in the infallibility of the Bible; we must first believe that every word is true—so many oracles of God. Therefore belief in the Bible is the first article in this creed —and this is a relapse into Judaism.

That this is a correct description of a good deal of our popular Christianity is evident to those who have given any attention to the popular as distinguished from the theological form of belief. The latter attempts to hold both the Bible and Christ at an equal level; in the popular religion the Bible is far above Christ. The extent to which the cause of Christianity is in the popular mind bound up with the very letter of our English version comes to us occasionally with a startling shock; as for instance, at the late revision of the Bible. A curious instance of the perseverance of the doctrine of biblical infallibility is afforded by one of the latest of modern " religions "—that of Tolstoi. He has no pity for the essential doctrines of Christianity; he throws to the winds the belief in Christ as we understand it; but the traditional view of the Bible is too strong even for this revolutionist to break through, and all unconsciously he builds his entire system upon it.

There is a remarkable parallel between the Jewish Pharisaism and this phase of Christianity. Slavery to the letter produced in both cases the same consequences: slavery to the past, the stiffening of religion into inflexible rigour and the numbness of conscience to present issues. Jesus found the bitterest opposition not from outside, but from religion itself; and if the spirit of Christ, which in these centuries has been active in emancipating man from one and another form of servitude and so has led to a higher civilisation, has often met with the stoutest opposition from those who stood as the representatives of his religion, it has been because Christianity like Judaism had largely degenerated into bibliolatry.

It is not, therefore, in the interests of a so-called "liberality" that we reject the treatment of the Bible as an infallible oracle, but because, being utterly baseless, that view is to-day the most fruitful cause of infidelity and one of the most serious obstacles to the advancement of the kingdom of God.

We were led into this discussion, partly to state and justify the foundation upon which the argument has proceeded, but mainly to find an answer to the question: What is the final authority in Christian ethics? We have found that the theory which ascribes infallible authority to the Bible is untenable and mischievous. This is a negative answer. We must now proceed to find the positive answer to our question, and for this purpose we turn to Christ. There can be no doubt what he recognized as the final authority: "My meat is to do the will of him that sent me." The one deepest principle of his life was obedience to the Father; he was ever listening to the divine voice; that was his guide. So, too, he taught his disciples to look above for guidance. In the last discourse his words were about the Holy Ghost and about prayer: "Whatsoever ye shall ask the Father in my name, he will give it you" (St. John, xvi. 23). With such prophecies and promises are intermingled other words which refer to himself:

"I am with you alway, even unto the end of the world" (St. Matt. xxviii. 20). And we must not forget how often he recurs to the subject of prayer: he taught his disciples to pray; he told them of God's care for them; he taught them to go to God as to a father who could give only good things to his sons; he instructed them to importune God in prayer.

In this teaching we recognise that truth which the old theologies embodied in the doctrine of Christ "in statu exaltationis." It is the truth that Christianity is not only a memory but a present fact; that the king still lives; that there is an infallible authority—God in heaven—who is accessible, who has promised to hear prayer and to be our guide. Is it not right that the truth of the headship of Christ in his Church should be brought out from the obscurity into which it has fallen? The kingdom of God is the greatest fact of history; every step of man towards a higher, fuller realisation of his destiny is a step towards the consummation of the kingdom of God; the secular coincides with the religious ideal, and the human race is seen to be moving forward in fulfilment of the end that Christ foresaw and in obedience to the laws which he set in operation. And the founder and leader of that kingdom is not a dimly-seen figure speaking to us from the distant past through the medium of a book, but a present power, a guide, who cannot and will not leave his work incomplete.

It must not be thought that this truth does away with the Bible; very far from it. But it does make the greatest difference whether we recognise Christ first and the Bible because of Christ, or the reverse. If Christ is first, then our faith does not depend upon the exact truth of every word of the Scriptures; but it may still be " a lamp unto our feet, and a light unto our path." We reverence it, though it is to us only a means to an end. We learn to believe that God has designed the preservation of the book for us and that it contains what is essentially a faithful picture of the life of the Saviour. Therefore we use it for our edification; but we recognise no truth that runs contrary to that other revelation of God in heart and conscience. God's living voice is supreme. We believe that God speaks to each individual. We hear him, sometimes in the earthquake, sometimes in the fire, but most often in the still small voice. The Christian's last court of appeal is neither the Bible, nor the pope, nor a supposed inner light, but God in heaven.

A great deal is said against " private judgment." It is maintained that the regulation of the Christian life must not be left to private judgment. There is a certain justice in the objection. The danger is that our own caprice will be taken for God's will. This delusion has led to many excesses in the history of the Christian Church. But these excesses have been owing, not to the use, but to a gross abuse of private judgment. The mistake has been in confusing two things: God's will, and the manifestation of that will in heart and conscience. The abuses of individual caprice are impossible where the distinction is kept in view, where the man holds before his mind God's will as separate from his own, and humbly listens for the manifestation of that will.

Under another aspect, the objection to private judgment is senseless. If man is not to use his judgment, then there is no reason why he should believe in Christianity any more than in Buddhism, or Atheism, or anything else that another tells him to believe in. To try to get away from private judgment as the last appeal to the only faculty that any human being ever had by which to rule his conduct is a thoughtless absurdity.

The lust of infallibility is the common mark of weak minds and has in our own generation led many to listen to the siren-voice of the Church of Rome. But those who understand God's intention in regard to man, not that he should be coddled into comfortable security, but that by the discipline of a faith in the unseen and eternal he should grow into approved, independent, virile character; who recognise character, not safety against an angry Deity, to be the end of religion, will find no allurement in a claim which pretends to share in the alone infallible authority of Almighty God. Whoever makes such a claim makes it not in the spirit of Christ, but in the spirit of the world.

We therefore recognise God as the ultimate authority for our ethical life. We believe that God speaks to us through our conscience, our reason, and also through the Bible rationally used. And in this fact, that the Christian's last authority is not a rigid rule, but a living God, we have an explanation of what otherwise would seem an anomaly in the Christian religion: the variableness of its ethics. What appears as a defect is in reality an evidence of the divine character of the kingdom of God. As man becomes more receptive and more capable of understanding the truth, the Christian ideal becomes higher. The truth in God remains the same; only man varies. To-day he has a deeper insight into the truth than he had a thousand years ago; therefore the ethical standard is so much higher, the conception of Christian character is so much fuller. New light is ever pouring in upon man. God uses every means to reveal truth to him: science, literature; even war, famine, pestilence; the genius of great men, the institutions of the state and philanthropy, the patient research of the scholar, the intuition of poet and seer: all and every one of these forces tend to make his moral sight clearer and to reveal to him more of the eternal law of God.

We can see, as we look over the Christian centuries, how different ages mark different steps in that fuller realisation of Christian truth. The first age of the Church was the age of the martyrs, and the resignation and willingness to suffer, virtues which the circumstances of that time called forth, have remained to this day indelibly stamped upon the Christian character.

It may, indeed, be questioned whether that particular element of character which was produced in the age of martyrs has not maintained too exclusive prominence in our ideas of Christian manhood. The conception of the Christian saint is still preëminently one who suffers. It is formed upon the ideal of him who "was brought as a lamb to the slaughter," who "when he was reviled, reviled not again." The preponderating influence of the martyr-type obscures other elements in the character of Christ and effects a certain onesidedness of Christian ideal. The sainthood of resignation is still held in higher honour than the sainthood of action.

As we follow the history of the Christian Church from the first beginnings we observe a continually enlarging Christian ideal. Its steps are marked by the care of the sick and the poor, in which Christian sympathy found its earliest expression; by the intellectual enthusiasm of the Renaissance, which has left an indelible mark upon the life of the Church; by the rise of the modern state, which bears perhaps the strongest testimony of all to the influence of Christian ideals; by the re-awakening of missionary enthusiasm.

In our time we are witnessing a change in the accepted views of life slowly coming over Christendom, the effect of Christ's teaching of the value of the individual. We see in the wonderful system of modern philanthropy, in the devotion with which men with no expectation of reward are giving their best efforts for the welfare and happiness of their fellowmen, signs that our ethical conceptions are being enlarged. We recognise this in the most striking social phenomenon of our time, that great movement extending to every Christian land, which constitutes what we call "the social problem." We cannot fail to note the connection between all the various phases of this agitation, by whatever name they call themselves, from Russian Nihilism to the mildest form of Christian Socialism. And, whatever we may think of it; however we may deplore the excesses to which it has led; however severely we may condemn the blindness of those who are looking to a revolution as the condition of a better future, and the light-hearted manner in which ignorance meddles with economic principles which specialists have to work hard to master: still we cannot fail to recognise that the secret spring of this world-wide movement is the recognition of the truth taught by Christ eighteen hundred years ago, of the value of the human soul simply because it is human. We must take the evil with the good; every breaking forth of the stream of human progress has its eddying backward currents. The life of to-day with its intense energy is just as much a product of Christianity on its dark as on its bright side. And the truth of the infinite value of the human soul, with its corollary, the equality of all men before God, may manifest itself in rough ways; but the incendiarism of anarchy as well as the devotion of philanthropy are signs that a new idea is taking hold of Christendom. They are the birth-throes of a larger conception of Christian character.

CHAPTER VIII.

THE KINGDOM OF GOD AND THE STATE.

✓ EXPANSION is the law of Christian ethics. This expansion is more striking in our day than it ever was. The " enthusiasm of humanity " has touched Christianity with aspirations for a more Christlike life, and is filling out the ideal of Christian manhood. We are learning to know Christ better and there is being formed a higher conception of the Christian.

It is at this point that we most clearly see the connection between Christian doctrine and Christian ethics. The doctrine of biblical infallibility, in itself untrue and a denial of the authority of Christ, has clouded the ideas of right and wrong. It has judaised Christianity by setting law in the central place of religion, and in so doing it has obscured and perverted the very fundamental and essential principle of Christian morality. It has blinded the eyes of men to the highest distinction of Christ's teaching. It has dwarfed and distorted the Christian ideal. It has changed that which came into the world as a command into a prohibition. It has put the negative for the positive.

When Christianity shall at last have freed itself from Jewish legalism, returned to Christ, and come to a clearer appreciation of the liberty of the gospel, then the negative conception of Christian ethics will make way for a truer appreciation of the possibilities of Christian character. The conception of Christian duty has been largely of what we are not to do; a deeper insight will bring with it this insistent appeal to the conscience: What as a Christian am I bound to do? When the law holds the central place in religion, religious duty exhausts itself in a struggle against doing wrong. The very essence and high prerogative of Christianity is that it leads us out of that prison-house. Over against the prohibition "thou shalt not" it sets the command: " Thou shalt love God and thy neighbour." It lifts man out of the brooding, morbid self-contemplation, where the energies of the soul are bent upon watching against sin, where the mind becomes entangled in hopeless casuistry and the best part of the man, his aspirations, are stifled, into the purer atmosphere of Christian duty, where the heart is filled and the evil spirit does not find it empty, swept, and garnished, where sin and wrong-doing are conquered by the desire and the recognised duty of doing right. When a man learns to put Christ above law, then he understands that Christian ethics is a positive command, that only by doing the will of God shall he know whether the doctrine is true; that he shall be saved, not by standing still and looking on and selfishly thinking only of keeping his hands clean, but by taking up arms in the warfare of life, by delivering good, honest blows for right and truth.

This is what we are coming to recognise, the new light that Christianity is gaining in our own age: the Christian ideal is a positive, aggressive ideal. In place of the terror of the law, there is a new motive: the sense of responsibility. I am here not for myself, not even to save my own soul; I dare not live my life for my own selfish gratification, not even if, like the anchorite of old, I spend my time in the wilderness or in a cave fighting the devil—a refined selfishness. I am placed here to do my part of the world's work, to fulfill that duty which God assigns to me in the working out of the kingdom of God. This is the bond that is to unite men in the brotherhood of one common purpose, this the end set to the Christian aspiration. Christianity draws men out; it touches the spring which is the strongest motive power in the human breast: the aspiration of the soul for the high and pure, the desire for that which is better, the longing for an ideal:

"We needs must love the highest when we see it."

Often and often that longing has been misdirected. We recognise it in mediæval monasticism, in the enthusiasm of the crusades, and in modern social movements. However misapplied, it is a deep-seated desire for a something beyond and above. It is this longing, this power of enthusiasm, this aspiration, which Christ takes hold of, directs, and guides into the fulfilment of God's will. Whoever remains untouched by some breath of this aspiration, whoever stays imprisoned in the spiritual thraldom of the letter, and persists in groping about among negative conceptions where sin always means some wrong done, but never the good left undone: he remains a stranger to the true spirit of Christianity.

The law of positive duty, of a personal responsibility for something to be done, is the essential ethical principle of Christianity in distinction from Judaism. And with this great principle there comes its necessary corollary: the law of proportional responsibility. In the parable of the talents, the lesson is not that all should bring the same amount, but that each should do according to his ability, and the man that brought but two talents received equal praise with him who brought the five. Every man is responsible in proportion to what he has received, or as Christ expresses it, in words which this generation would do well to heed and ponder: " Unto whomsoever much is given, of him shall be much required" (St. Luke, xii. 48).

Just here we have still most to learn. In that blending of tones which should form the harmony of the Christian character, this one note is still missed. True, there are many who, gifted with many talents, are striving to the best of their ability that their last account may be a good one, recognising the superior responsibility which superior gifts bring with them, and they are rightly esteemed as the noblest exponents of Christianity. But that principle of proportional responsibility has not yet entered as an element into the common popular estimation of character. The most finished production of eighteen hundred years of Christianity is the Christian gentleman. The Christian gentleman must be pure, courteous, high-minded, generous. But the Christian gentleman is a very negative character. The popular conception has not yet risen to the height of the Christian ideal. The Christian gentleman must do no wrong; but it is not demanded of him that he should be aggressively good. There is a note left out. The positive side of Christianity, the sense of proportional responsibility, of a duty which is so much greater because of the many gifts: this is largely or wholly unrepresented in the highest conception popularly formed of Christian character. The Christian gentleman is what his name denotes, a gentle creature; that is a high virtue, but Christianity demands something more virile, more energetic, more positive.

Here then we may expect a forward movement in Christian ethical conception. What has been accomplished by Christianity is truly wonderful. It has substituted for the ancient ideal of manhood a pattern which the Greek or Roman would have laughed to scorn. But it will do much more. It will fill out that ideal. The light of God which never ceases to shine will enlarge men's conceptions. Christianity will build up its own pattern into nobler proportions. The Christian gentleman of the future will be one who has within him the true spirit of chivalry, the spirit which makes men strong to do battle for right and justice. In the coming generations no man will be able to lay claim to the proud title of gentleman, who wastes his time either in trivial amusements or respectable idleness; who, whatever his courtesy or refinement, is a mere drone in society; who does not remember that what he calls his own is God's, and only given him that he should use it wisely for himself and his fellow-men. No man will be accounted a gentleman who does not do his part of the world's work, any more than to-day a man is called a gentleman who would strike a woman.

Human customs and institutions in an imperfect way often embody Christian ideas. And herein they illustrate both the unquenchable aspirations of humanity, and man's weakness in realising these aspirations. So we trace in one historic institution a foreshadowing of that Christian sense of responsibility which is now beginning to affect the popular estimation of character. When you have stripped the idea of aristocracy of its adventitious elements, the pride of birth, of power, position, wealth;—what remains as its kernel is the Christian idea of proportional responsibility. Aristocracy, so far as it has real meaning and value, is an attempt at embodying in actual fact the Christian principle that the more a man has, so much the more he owes. Hence the French saying: *noblesse oblige*.[1] It is no foolish dream—for it is already in process of realisation—that Christianity in America, where we are freed from the prescriptive conventional glamour of birth or title, shall produce a purer aristocracy, whose only

[1] Compare the Prince of Wales's motto: " Ich dien."

title is that a man makes return in service according to what God has given him; whose distinction is the consciousness that every blessing of God, good parents, education, position, wealth, and Christian privileges, adds just so much more to responsibility, and where the sense of a duty owed becomes the inspiring motive of life.

The two principles which I have here endeavoured to emphasise as characterising that enlargement of Christian ethical conceptions which is taking place—a positive as distinguished from a negative morality, and a responsibility proportioned to individual gifts and advantages—will be found to have an immediate application to the great problems which are at present agitating the civilised world. First of these is the so-called " social question."

I have already spoken of the present universal social agitation and unrest as a phenomenon which has the closest connection with Christianity. It is not surprising, therefore, that we find the Church absorbed in the keenest interest for this movement and a very widespread sympathy for its objects.

It is true that we have to deplore a frequent lack of discrimination on the part of the Church and especially the clergy, who are inclined to go beyond the sphere which is properly theirs and trespass upon a domain where they are not at home and where their well-intentioned ignorance is often the cause of great mischief. Economics and theology are mutually exclusive departments of human knowledge; and when the representative of religion pronounces judgment upon such questions as wages, the influence of trusts, etc., he is liable to expose himself to the ridicule of the trained economist, who has devoted years of exclusive study to these problems and who has learned reverence for the laws governing the social relations, which the theologian is apt to overlook in light-hearted unconsciousness.

The socialistically-tinged Christianity of our day is from one point of view a most encouraging sign. As such it represents a timely revolt from what Matthew Arnold called

> "The barren optimistic sophistries
> Of comfortable moles."

It shows that the Church is still quick to respond to the wants of the time, that it has a feeling for that aspiration which is the legitimate moving power of the universal social movement. For there can be no doubt that the object of socialism is a noble one, and one which closely coincides with the Christian ideal, and that the present unrest does point to a radical wrong in the relationship between men. But, in the lack of perception of the true nature of the wrong, by the want of discrimination in the use of means to right the wrong, socialistic Christianity threatens to become a grave danger, and to work incalculable harm to the cause of the poor which it has espoused.

What we see going on is, indeed, nothing less than a recrudescence of the old conflict between religion and science. Science showed that the sudden creations and rapid transformations which religion, forsaking her proper sphere, had postulated were impossible, that God works with the utmost slowness and deliberation by immutable laws towards his end. A new science has shown the same deliberation, the same immutability, in another sphere, in the working of economic laws towards the elevation of mankind. And again representatives of religion rebel against that slowness and immutability. But the new conflict will react much more harmfully upon religion than the old.

It is, however, becoming increasingly evident that the solution of the great social question must be sought in the moral sphere and can only be reached by improvement in character. Here is the Church's opportunity. But she must stand on her own ground and not meddle where she is an intruder. Christianity has a message for the social wants of our day, and if I might venture a prediction, I should say that the key to the situation will be found in the Christian principle of proportional responsibility: " Unto whomsoever much is given, of him shall be much required."

The other great problem with which the Church stands in closest relations is that of the state.

We cannot but recognise the guiding hand of Providence in that process by which the laws of human partnership have been evolved from the earliest time to the present: the tribe, the monarchy, the empire, the modern state. The last in the line of development, the state as we know it represents a new principle in the social life. Arising out of the break-up of the Roman Empire, the modern state came on the scene when the leaven of Christianity had permeated the masses and had given reality to the ethical life. It is this ethical life, possible only through Christianity, that in turn made possible the modern state. And the state is the great ethical problem of our day.

John Stuart Mill, in his essay on Liberty, charges Christianity with a defect in failing to provide rules for the Christian's duty to the state. The charge witnesses to a misunderstanding of the true nature of Christianity. For the very distinction of our religion is that it provides no rules for individual cases—how could Christ make rules for a condition of things which was not then present, of which his disciples could have no faintest conception?—but that it establishes the fundamental principle of ethics and implants in men the moral imperative to make the application of that principle to each new condition. But there is a certain justice in the charge, if it is taken as directed, not against the religion, but against the representatives of the religion. For perhaps the most serious ethical defect of our modern Christianity is that it fails to realise its own sponsorship for the state.

There have been at various times efforts to shape the national life in accordance with the law of Christ. But the mediæval papacy and Puritanism, which stand as the most noted representatives of these efforts, embody a principle thoroughly different from that which we to-day recognise as embodied in the state. The highest conception to which these systems attained was characterised by a certain externality and forcefulness. The state in itself was neither to the mediæval Catholic nor to the Puritan a divine creation. As an element of the world, it was to be subdued to the law of Christ. It stood over against the Church, and by receiving the Church's yoke it was to be made the handmaid of the Church.

The modern state stands upon a different footing. It claims, as well as the Church, the distinction of a divine ordination. It shares with the Church something of the latter's prerogative; it is in a sense co-equal with the Church. There has been committed to it, as to the Church, a share of the divine work for man. It has a part in the mission to humanity. It is the sphere within which man exercises those virtues which fit him for the future kingdom.

There is, therefore, a necessary organic relation between the state and the kingdom of God, and we shall now be in a position to define that relation. The kingdom of God is God's ultimate end and purpose for the human race. We cannot ascribe to the state the same permanence. But, if we read the lesson of history aright, it is God's will that his kingdom should in this our time embody itself in the state. The ideal of the state as we now understand it, the democratic state, is on its ethical side identical with the ideal of the kingdom of God, as confined to any particular area. The conditions required for the kingdom are essential for the full realisation of the state. Undoubtedly, the state and with it patriotism are destined to pass away and give place to a higher conception of corporate unity, where all barriers shall disappear before the sentiment of one common humanity. But we are presumably very far from that end. At the present time the state comprehends within itself the highest ideal of the common ethical life of humanity. The state is, as it were, a segment of the kingdom of God as it exists in our time, in an imperfect condition, in a state of growth.

No lower conception of the office and sphere of the state will fit in with a Christian view of the world. However imperfect the life of the state appears now, we do not discover its true character in its condition at any one moment of time, any more than we can understand the nature of the kingdom of God from a view of it at any single moment of its history. As with the kingdom, so with the state: its essential principle is growth, aspiration, expansion. We believe that it is the divinely appointed means, for the era in which we live, towards the realisation of the kingdom of God.[1] When the means shall have served its purpose it will doubtless be discarded. But that does not impair the reality

[1] It was the merit of De Tocqueville to have clearly recognised the religious foundation of American nationality.—See *Democracy in America*.

of those large and high ideals for which the state at present stands. It is an actuality for us and it is for us to recognise its divine character.

We can now also understand the relation between the Church and the state. They both work together for the same appointed end: the consummation of the kingdom of God. Each has its own sphere; each contributes its own portion to the common object. It is the special function of the Church to lay the religious foundation; religion, the direct relation of man to God, is its particular sphere. The state furthers the ethical life of the kingdom. The ordering of the mutual relationships of men in human society upon the basis of the divine law is the function of the state. So we understand the Church and the state to be fellow-workers in solving the problem of humanity.

It is one of the shortcomings of our present-day Christianity that it does not recognise this relationship between the kingdom of God and the state. The Church is wanting in the sense of responsibility towards the state. The fatal delusion of an earthly infallibility has imposed upon her a crystalline rigour and robbed her of the adaptability which, recognising the hand of Providence in the changes of the world, brings forth " out of her treasure things new and old " to meet these changes. God has cast human society into new forms. In the richness of the Christian treasure are the principles which are essential to the preservation of these forms. But the Church rarely brings them forth.

Christian people have been somewhat in the habit of satisfying their public obligations by finding fault. There is a certain useless indulgence in tirades against the evils of the times. Lurid pictures are drawn of the degradation of our public life. We have had such jeremiads *ad nauseam*. Is it not time that Christian energy were directed to pointing out those principles whose application to the existing conditions shall promise relief?

Our estimate of these conditions will vary according to the point of view from which we regard them. The first question here refers to the object for which the state exists. It is one of those comfortable doctrines whose truth is tacitly assumed, the unconscious postulate of argument, that the state exists for the well-being and comfort of the individual. It is the power which regulates social life, to the end of personal peace and satisfaction. Our considerations of the state in its relation to the kingdom of God have prepared us to recognise another purpose. The modern state exists for the production of character. A battle-ground of character, a field for the exercise and building up of manly virtue: this is the meaning of the state as understood from the Christian point of view.

The Christian, therefore, faces the situation with a sense of duty. He brings to the task something more than inherited prejudices, time-worn sophistries, and platitudes which pass for reasons. Its exigencies are to him a call, not for criticism or unavailing lamentation, but for the discharge of a sacred duty in the investigation and application of those principles which are essential to the furtherance of the national life.

This task is not a difficult one, when we have recognised the distinguishing characteristic of Christian morality. The state cannot exist upon the negative principles of Hebrew ethics, but demands that its citizens bring to it that sense of positive duty which recognises a responsibility proportioned to the individual's gifts. The Christian state finds its ethical correlate in the Christian principle of proportional responsibility.

This principle puts a different face upon the situation, and corrects some inveterate prejudices. It is one of the axiomatic pre-conceptions, received everywhere as current coin, that the ills of our public life are due to the inert mass of ignorant, low, venal and vicious humanity, which hangs like a dead weight upon our free institutions, and that universal suffrage is the monumental failure of our day. But once realise the bearing of the Christian principle of a proportional responsibility, which exacts not the same from all alike, but so much more as your gifts are larger, and let it be understood that the state exists largely for the elevation of that corrupt mass of ignorance and viciousness: and the responsibility will be seen to lie elsewhere.

For many centuries, perhaps as far back as the knowledge of human affairs extends, liberty has been the goal of human progress. Many battles have been fought in the long warfare of advancing civilisation in behalf of social and political freedom. Liberty has been in all ages the watchword which filled the human breast with enthusiasm and inspired deeds of heroism. One barrier after another has been overthrown which stood in the way of the untrammelled expansion of personal and political life.

What still remains to be done ? What will be the next issue about which the battle will be drawn ? We ask that question and we look in vain for an answer. With us Americans at least, the battle of liberty has been fought to a finish. As far as we are concerned, liberty is a dead issue. The equality of man is an accomplished fact; there is no more tyranny, no oppression; there are no unnatural impediments, no impassible barriers. Freedom is complete. The cry of liberty no longer appeals to us, it stirs no more noble emotions.

Shall we, therefore, say that the battle of progress and civilisation has been fought? that we can now rest on our laurels ? By no means. We can see gathering on the horizon the dark clouds of coming storms. We seem to be hurrying onward towards new crises which will be as eventful and as full of difficulty as any which mark the past progress of the human race. But whoever would face the new issues and solve the problems of the future, must put aside the rusty weapons of the past and arm himself anew for the fight.

The truth which in one generation is the seed-corn of a great and beneficent revolution becomes in the next a falsehood stopping the wheels of progress. Equality was once the grandest of truths. But to-day it has become a falsehood, which its blind votaries place in the way of human advance. Men are not equal: this is the truth upon whose recognition hinges the further progress of civilisation. The man who has a thousand is not the same as the man who has a hundred; the man who has gone through college is not the same as he who has barely learned to read and write; the man who has been brought up with careful nurture is not the same as the man whose father and mother were drunkards; and the man who enjoys the inestimable privileges of Christianity is not the same as the man who, for whatever reason, is a stranger to them.

Our judgments of the present and our outlook into the future will radically differ according as we recognise or do not recognise these differences and the differences in responsibility that go with them. I cannot see how there can be two opinions as to what Chistianity teaches. It recognises the principle of proportional responsibility. From the Christian point of view there can be no doubt as to where the responsibility for the political evils of the present lies. "Unto whomsoever much is given, of him shall be much required." With the many splendid exceptions which we delight to honour and which promise a better future, we cannot conceal from ourselves that it is the selfishness of wealth, of education, of refinement, of Christianity, which to-day is the greatest barrier to progress. Not until men shall learn the Christian principle of property, that it is held in stewardship for God, not until they learn the Christian principle of responsibility, which requires for every advantage and blessing from God a service to fellowmen, shall we realise any approach to that higher and better social life in the state for which God has destined us.

The saddest sight in our land to-day is not the corruption of public officers or the ignorance of the masses, but the selfishness of those who ought to know better, but who prefer their private advantage to the public good: the many thousands of the well to do, of the educated, of professedly Christians, who have never lifted one finger or spoken one word for purity and honesty in public life. What Theodore Parker wrote when the dark cloud of slavery hung over the nation is precisely true to-day: "If our educated men had done their duty, we should not now be in the ghastly condition we bewail."[1]

No prophet ever uttered truer words than those spoken by George William Curtis in 1883: "While good men sit at home, not knowing that there is anything to be done, nor caring to know; cultivating a feeling that politics are tiresome and dirty, and politicians vulgar bullies and bravoes; half persuaded that a republic is the contemptible rule of a mob, and secretly longing for a splendid and vigorous despotism—then remember it is not a government mastered by ignorance, it is a goverment betrayed by intelligence; it is not the victory of the slums, it

[1] Quoted by G. W. Curtis, lecture on "Political Infidelity."

is the surrender of the schools; it is not that bad men are brave, but that good men are infidels and cowards."[1]

"Good men are infidels:" it is a just charge against the infidelity of our modern Christianity. For the burden of responsibility lies upon the Church. Why are these things possible in a Christian society? How is it that men still enjoy the reputation of being good men and Christians who have never performed one duty to society? Why, moreover, is it that a man may sink the public welfare in subserviency to party, or condone dishonest practices in public life, and yet hold his head high in a Christian society? We are constrained to answer: The Church has not yet learned to appreciate her obligation or her opportunity. The Church has the power of affecting public opinion so as to bring scorn and contempt upon the man who performs no duty to the public or who allows selfishness to dictate his course. It is upon the Christianity of the country that in the last resort rests the responsibility for the immoral condition of our public life. That Christianity has not yet fully awakened either to the con-

[1] Speech made before the New England Society on "Puritan Principle and Puritan Pluck." It is impossible not to feel keenly the destructive tendencies in modern society, how the laboriously achieved progress of our modern civilisation is threatened by the socialistic agitation. But it is equally impossible for the candid observer, admitting the justice of the position taken in the text, to deny that this danger is but the nemesis for the neglect by Christianity and the Church of the Christian principle of a responsibility proportioned to the individual's gifts. God's justice often works out its ends in rough ways.

sciousness of the true relation of the state to the kingdom of God, or to the Christian principle of a proportional responsibility, in which that relation must find its practical realisation.

The Church of Christ to-day holds the key to the situation. There are not wanting signs that she is coming more fully to realise her mission. It is becoming more and more recognised that the duty of the citizen to the state opens up to the vigour and enthusiasm of the Church a sphere for putting Christian principles into action, where every effort tells towards the expansion of the kingdom of God. It is not too much to hope that we are on the threshold of a time when the ethical conceptions of Christendom, whose gradual expansion in the past makes the history of civilisation, will receive an enlargement. It will come slowly. And its realisation will effect a change in civilised society which will find a parallel only in that softening of manners which made the gladiatorial shows impossible. Never was given to the Church a grander opportunity for serving God and man. A thoughtful realisation of God's will for man, which shall make her see the God-ordained mission of the state, and a strength of purpose to perform her allotted function: let her fulfill these conditions, and she will rise to her splendid opportunity.

The task, we cannot conceal from ourselves, is a great one: it is nothing less than the creation of a new sense in the mass of humanity. It exists in a few; the sense of proportional responsibility is what gives a touch of splendour to the noblest lives. Shall we look upon these as the anomalies? a kind of freak of nature, which we cannot explain? No. It is the many, lacking that sense of responsibility, who are the anomalies. The men who to-day live in the fear of God, for the service of man, counting all things God's, nothing theirs: these are the true exponents of Christianity. It is idle to dream that we shall ever reach perfection. But it is the anomalous self-contradictory state of our present-day Christianity, that men are walking about who perform no duty to the state or fellowman, and yet who are allowed to cherish the delusion that they are Christians and civilised. This is simply the contradiction of Christianity. To say that this is the state with which we must rest satisfied, with a thankful acknowledgment of the few brilliant exceptions, but still allowing them to be by right exceptions: this is to have a very low opinion of the power of Christianity.

History, on the contrary, bears unmistakable testimony to the tremendous influence of that spiritual force which entered the world with Christ; and when we consider what Christianity has done we shall be careful in drawing the line at what Christianity can do. The first thought or sentiment which Christianity infused into men was that of the sacredness of human life. Any one who had lived in the days of ancient Rome, when deformed children were exposed and the lord was master of the slave's life, could have had little conception of the change that would come; and if a prophet had then foretold the stringency of our laws for the protection of human life, if he had drawn a picture of a modern hospital to an ancient Roman, he would have been laughed at as a visionary, just as "practical" men to-day laugh at the visionaries who believe in the power of ideal forces.

Moreover, Christianity has a power of unfolding itself. The light has constantly increased. Long after that first lesson, the sacredness of life, had been learned, there dawned upon the Christian consciousness that other truth—the infinite value of the human soul, with the dignity which it gives to all life. And if a fairy's wand could reproduce from the past of five hundred years ago some English, German, or French community, and put it down side by side with an American community of to-day under similar circumstances, the contrast would be almost as striking as that between heathenism and Christianity.

When we consider what Christianity has done, we shall not despair of what Christianity can do. We shall believe that Christianity may yet change the last vestige of savagery, the readiness to fight, into the Christian virtue of readiness to serve. We shall believe that the Church has it in her power so to shape public sentiment that a man will be branded as contemptible and made a social outcast, who does not perform some service to his fellowmen in some way commensurate to the gifts which God has bestowed upon him.

We have been led to these reflections by a consideration of the ethical determination of the Christian life. We found that the only infallible authority for the Christian is God. With the acknowledgment of this truth the field is open for an indefinite ethical expansion. The Christian life is made up of the two elements—the religious and the ethical. Its ideal is twofold: peace with God and obedience to his will. No life is normal without either of these. And if we understand the meaning of Christ aright, it is the realisation of that twofold ideal of life under his own leadership that is comprehended under the idea of the kingdom of God.

It remains to set the kingdom of God in its true historic light by showing its relation to one of the greatest facts of modern history, itself also the embodiment of an idea. The kingdom of God finds its historic antithesis in the kingdom of the pope. By this is meant, that if the kingdom of God is the realisation in human life of Christ's intention and promises the elevation of humanity to the highest attainable heights, the modern papacy is that organisation which in our day presents the greatest obstacle to the advancement of that kingdom. I say advisedly, the modern papacy, because the papacy of this century, as it has developed since that 24th day of May, 1814, when Pius VII. returned to Rome, is a very different thing from the papacy as it was before.

The papacy is not the Church of Rome, though it has almost sucked the vitality out of that body. The Church of Rome is a body comprising a vast number of human souls, in which lives much beautiful piety and devotion, but where whatever there is of true religion exists in spite of the iron hand of a system which is doing its best to throttle all spiritual life. The papacy is the child of the ancient Cæsarism. It is supposed by some to be a religious organisation; it is as truly mundane as the Cæsarism whose mantle it has assumed. It is a vast and wonderful system with one head, whose essential governing principle is the exploitation of the religious interests of its followers for its own worldly benefit. The lust of rule is the secret of the papacy, as it was the principle of Roman imperialism.

One of the most singular phenomena of our modern intellectual life is the almost total indifference of accurate research to that great power, the papacy.[1] There is no fact of heaven or earth that is not to-day subjected to the closest scrutiny of the keenest minds, be it of the physical constitution of the world or of history. Every line of investigation in every department of knowledge is followed with the most intense interest. But here is one of the colossal phenomena of history, a world-wide empire comprising a vast multitude, every individual of whom recognises above the secular authority of his particular state the authority of the head of that empire;

---

[1] The attention given on our side to the papal bull on Anglican orders is a mortifying sign of the degeneration of Protestantism. Half the argument is yielded to the pope by taking him seriously. I do not undervalue orders ; but Protestantism is untrue to itself if it does not hold the Church of Christ at a higher value than these hair-splitting distinctions.

and in our own time his claim to divine attributes has been allowed and accepted. And yet this great fact excites little attention. Our modern investigator looks with contempt upon superstition. It does not occur to him that superstition, as well as any other fact, requires an explanation. Says Prof. Harnack, referring to the decrees of the Vatican Council : "Our century has accepted almost in silence what could have been offered to the spirit of no previous century, without rousing an armed Europe to battle, both Catholics and Protestants."[1]

This singular attitude of the modern intellectual world towards the papacy can, I think, be traced to two causes. The first of these is that exclusive tendency of Protestantism, which, identifying religion with intellectual problems, over these problems forgets the needs of millions of human creatures, who care nothing about intellectual questions, but who have very decided religious wants. The second is the strange blindness which prevails in the intellectual world to the religious factor. It is a common opinion that social man can be understood without taking into consideration the chief motives which govern the actions of the individual.

There is no more disastrous mistake than that which is frequently made, which, in classifying the forces that to-day are operative in society, places the destructive forces of atheism, infidelity, materialism, at the one extreme, and at the other the supposedly conservative force of a superstitious religion, and

[1] *Dogmengeschichte*, iii., p. 648.

which inclines to look upon that spirit which is credulous of everything and yields to any authority that calls itself religious as a fault leaning to virtue's side. History teaches abundantly that superstition and unbelief are close friends. They have more than once become allies, as they did under a Frederick II. and under a Napoleon. Prof. Harnack, speaking of modern France, shows how irreligion and Jesuitism have clasped hands: "The Huguenots had been expelled, the Jansenists broken or annihilated: the French people now belonged to the Encyclopedists and Voltaire. It hated the Jesuits; but because it is easy enough to drive out the fear of God, but not the terror of God, this people belonged from that time to that very Church of the Jesuits which it hated and derided.'[1]

The kingdom of God and the kingdom of the pope are antitheses, because the one, recognising the wants innate in human nature, brings man to his Creator; the other, recognising those same wants, by them leads man to the usurped throne of a creature. The end of the kingdom of God is God, the end of the papacy is the pope. This distinction designates the two poles of human character: that which looks above the creature to the eternal and is fast anchored in God, and that which does not rise above earth and is anchored in the shifting sands of human mutability.

It is no mere accident, but an entirely natural consequence of the essential nature of state and

[1] *Ibid.*, iii., p. 639.

Church, that the history of Europe in this century is largely the history of an intense struggle between the aspiring sense of nationality and the papacy, and that even in America we have an uneasy feeling of an approaching storm. By the conditions of its being the Church of Rome is irreconcilably opposed to the modern state. The democratic state is founded upon the principles of the gospel, it is the embodiment of the kingdom of God; and the papacy, which, by setting the pope in the place of God, has repudiated the gospel, has instinctively recognised in the spirit of nationality its enemy, with whom there can be only a life and death struggle.

One may stand in Rome upon the Pincian Hill. The eternal city at his feet is overshadowed by the vast pile of St. Peters and the Vatican. Opposite, at one of the highest points of the surrounding hills, overlooking the city, is the heroic equestrian statue of Garibaldi. Outlined against the sky it is a striking feature of the landscape—and as suggestive as it is striking. He stands there as having come to conquer and rule over the city at his feet. In that statue I seemed to see the spirit of nationality and the kingdom of God come to conquer, not in Italy only, but the world over, the kingdom of him who has usurped the place of God. So, we believe, it is written in the decrees of heaven.

THE END